# THE BANJO!

## A DISSERTATION,

BY

## S. S. STEWART,

Author of "THE COMPLETE AMERICAN BANJO SCHOOL,'
" THE BANJO PHILOSOPHICALLY," ETC., ETC.

PHILADELPHIA, PENN'A.

S. S. STEWART,
No. 223 Church Street.

J. S. Stewart.

3

# DEDICATION.

---

To the Banjoists of America,
And to those who are learning;
To those who aspire to the higher art—
To those within whom the Light is burning.
(That Light which lends to human beings the power of the Gods)
And to those who for greater knowledge are yearning.
To one and all, both rich and poor;
To the man of gall,—the unconscious boor.
To the little ones—ofttimes called great;
And also to those who the Banjo hate.
To the poor, because the book is cheap,
To the rich, because the volume's neat—
To him who reads and reading thinks;
To him who presses onward—never sinks.
To every student who wishes to learn,
And to all who perchance would attention turn
To THE BANJO, this little volume is faithfully inscribed, by

THE AUTHOR.

*Philadelphia, August,* 1888.

# "THE BANJO."

## A DISSERTATION

BY

### S. S. STEWART.

## PRIMARY OBSERVATIONS.

"A spiral winds from the worlds to the suns,
And every star that shines
In the path of degrees forever runs,
And the spiral octave climbs."

"There is no new thing under the sun." The inventions of the present day and age are but the echoes of similar contrivances used in past generations and bygone ages.

Ages before Columbus set foot on American soil—thousands of years before the untutored American Indian inhabited this Continent, there is little doubt that the land we now inhabit was the home of a vast civilization, and of a people that were, to say the least, as far advanced in many respects as we are to-day.

"History repeats itself." Sound moves in waves. Events are governed by cyclic laws. To-day is the to-morrow of yesterday. The future is linked with the past.

It is said that stringed instruments are almost    as old as the world." The Violin is traced by some writers as antedating the Christian Era many years, and doubtless the musicians of that age could have traced it backward many hundred years from thence.

With a few modifications, slight alterations and perhaps more or less brilliant variations, we are doing the same things over again which have been done long years ago.

> " The new is old, the old is new,
> The cycle of a change sublime,
> Still sweeping through ! "

The instrument known as the American Banjo to-day, is the result of an evolution from the primative instru ments used by the negroes of the South ; as the far fame( "three-string gourd" of Picaune Butler was the result of an involution from the more perfected musical instruments. For there can be no evolution without a parallel involution. "Light comes from the East" and returns again thereto.

The undeveloped mind of the negro received musical ideas from minds further advanced. He received them according to his developement and reflected them as his comprehension and mechanical skill permitted.

Hence, some have claimed that the instrument, now called the Banjo, is of negro origin.

And what if such were the case ? Truth has often come into the world through lowly channels  The stone which the builder rejects to-day, is made the corner-stone of the temple to-morrow.

The much despised and tabooed Banjo of past generations has become to-day the popular musical favorite of many cultivated people of America. To become acquainted with it—to become familiar with its many musical qualities—is to love it. And one has only to make himself acquainted with it to become its ardent admirer.

In spite of the adverse criticisms of bigoted and prejudiced minds, the Banjo has gone on gaining in popular favor. In spite of the many improperly constructed instruments of the Banjo class, forced upon the public notice, and often in the hands of unskilled performers, the instrument has made rapid progress and gained many new adherants. In spite of the fact that it has had to battle against the surging current of popular prejudice for many years, the Banjo stands before you to-day, reader, as demanding, yes, and commanding, notice from the advanced musical minds of the day.

It comes before you demanding the recognition it deserves. It will receive—it is receiving this recognition.

———

And now, as a past musical age gives up its dead to live again, the Banjo—one of which is said to have been discovered in the Egyptain Pyramids, blossoms again into life with the existing generation, and clothes itself in the form and garments of an American civilization.

It is with the present and future that we deal. We must therefore write of the Banjo of to-day, and of the American Banjo, as it is called; leaving the obscure and misty past to seek repose within the bosom of antiquity.

Those who find recompense only, and can delight in nothing else so much, may if they see fit continue to burrow in the earth and in the sea; in worm-eaten books, and more or less doubtful records of the past, for relics of the Banjo, as it was known to past ages, and extinct races; but it is with us now that the task of championing the Banjo of the present day and generation lies. This task has fallen, as a mantle, upon one who accepts it

gladly, perhaps; but gladly only because he has made,
through unceasing and untiring effort and application,
himself familiar with the many inherent musical beauties
of the instrument. He has delayed, from time to time,
placing before a critical public the observations in the
form herein displayed. He has waited only in the hope
that someone more competent than himself would take
up the subject, as outlined in his lecture, *The Banjo
Philosophically*, and give to the world a dissertation upon
the Banjo; but these fond hopes have not been realized,
nor does it appear that they are soon to be; hence, he
now offers to the reading public, and to the Banjoists of
America, this little work; at the same time making no
claim to literary skill; for how can one who is engaged
in active business, and meeting daily and hourly all the
annoyances that a person in mercantile life must put up
with, have time for literary culture? The reader is therefore asked to overlook any faults in style and expression,
and to kindly accept the work for what it is intended, and
to withhold judgment until the entire subject in hand has
been attentively read and considered.

**"Docendo Dicimus."**

# PREFACE.

Were it not for the literati, the Violin as a musical instrument would not hold the prominent place it holds to-day. Had there been no musical literature, the violin would doubtless have remained, to this day, a "fiddle" only, in the minds of the masses. Paganini might have drawn his bow in vain were it not for the musical press, which drew attention to the artist and his instrument. All great things have had small beginnings. The seed must be planted in the earth before the tree can come forth. "Out of the depths" have arisen much that is pure and good.

Shortly after publishing my lecture, called, for want of a more appropriate title, "*The Banjo Philosophically*," I received in my daily mail a letter from a gentleman whose name to-day is well and favorably known to many of my readers as the accomplished composer of some of the best music written for the banjo, and as the compiler and arranger of valuable musical works. The gentleman in question is no other than Mr. John H. Lee, and as his letter has been one of the principal causes which have led to the writing of this present work, I will, with the reader's permission, append a portion of it. The letter is dated on the 22d of September, 1886, and reads as follows:

"A perusal of your lecture entitled 'The Banjo Philosophically,' afforded me great pleasure. It is by far the best thing you have ever written on the Banjo.

and I know whereof I speak, because you have been
kind enough to forward me at all times your publications
as they were issued, and *I read them always.* I am not
one of the kind that curry favor by a judicious application of 'taffy,' nor do I think you are gullible enough to
be influenced by it, but I do believe in honest compliment; therefore I wish to convey to you my honest
appreciation of this, your latest. The scientific portion
of the work, you will admit, is of more interest to the
would-be manufacturer of the Banjo than to the expert
manipulator, who rarely cares to delve into its intricacies;
but the latter portion of the lecture, devoted to advice
and instruction regarding the care, playing and various
remarks concerning the Banjo, are of great interest to
ALL, student and professor, alike. A little more of the
same class of Banjo literature would elevate its standing
and force recognition from the few remaining bigots who
are prejudiced against the establishment of the Banjo as
" legitimate instrument.*

The Banjo needs all the good things that can be
written about it. There are few men with the requisite
knowledge of the Banjo that are devoted to it. There
are few with devotion that possess the requisite knowledge to aid its progress. Granting the requisite knowledge and devotion, the question of literary ability arises.
Many have developed the musical resources of the banjo

---

* "The Banjo Philosophically" was written during the summer of 1886, and now during the summer of 1888, at the time
when the young artist, Mr. D. C. Everest, who is studying music
in Paris, France, is making such a wonderfully favorable impression upon musical minds in that city, with his Banjo, I have set
myself again to the task of writing on the Banjo. What I
may be doing a summer another two years hence I of course do
not know, but hope that I shall not, at least, be regretting the
few hours spent in writing this dissertation.

by their compositions, but in the literary sense you have the field to yourself. Volumes have been written about other instruments, but the Banjo, with the exception of such articles as you have written for the *Journal*, has been neglected."

As I consider Mr. Lee a gentleman well qualified to judge as to the wants of the banjo-playing public and the student of the banjo, as well as one having long experience as a player of the banjo and other instruments, I should not hesitate to act upon any suggestion that he, or another of like qualification, should offer; and as an experience of two years since the issuing of *The Banjo Philosophically*, has not passed without giving me some additional knowledge of the subject, I have thought best to follow the lecture with the present *Dissertation*.

That the last two years have witnessed a great increase in the interest manifested in the banjo and banjo-playing there is no doubt; and that this interest will continue to increase as the beauties of the instrument become better known, no one can doubt. Many of our colleges and schools now contain numerous banjo players. "Banjo clubs" have entertained many at musical concerts given by students during the past year. In an article published in a recent number of " *Woman*," a monthly magazine, in relation to the Seaside Institute, of Bridgeport, Conn., it is stated that the class in Banjo playing numbered forty-two members during the season of 1887–8. Other institutions have similar classes. Musicians, who a few years ago tabooed the instrument, now begin to admire it. All over the country it is making itself known and becoming loved.

Without wishing to incur the charge of egotism, I will append an extract from a recent letter received from a

Southern gentleman; warm-hearted and impulsive, as many Southerners are, he was pleased and delighted with his purchase of a banjo. The gentleman is a Tennesseean, stockman and merchant—Will McMackin, by name. He writes as follows:

" I figure this way. The face is an index to the heart. Seventy-five per cent. of the poets I have seen, both men and women, are very handsome. Poetry is music—music is love. Love is a Heaven-born gift, engraved upon the heart with the fingers of God. Through your portrait in musical journals, the public have formed a very high appreciation of you. Your magnanimity in shipping a costly instrument minus C. O. D. bill, has made you the theme of much compliment and praise. In more ways than one I have cause to appreciate your letter."

Now I do not flatter myself that I am extremely handsome, but then, the old saying, " Handsome is as handsome does," may apply in my case. At any rate, the portraits of myself which have been published, have led many persons into the serious mistake of supposing me to be a large burly man—a veritable "slugger." This I am led to believe on account of numerous visitors, who when meeting me for the first time, have frequently addressed me in some such language as this—" You are an entirely different man from what I expected to see. I had an idea that you were a great big man, weighing about two hundred and fifty pounds."

I surely do not know where they could have gathered such an impression unless it was from the wood engravings representing my portrait. Therefore, that my readers may be better acquainted with me, I now make the remarks that I am rather small of stature and weigh about one hundred and thirty to one hundred and thirty-five pounds. I was born on the

eighth day of January, in the year 1855, and am therefore now a few months over thirty-three years of age.
My experience with the banjo *as a business*, extends over
a period of some ten years. Previous to this, I studied
music and the banjo as an amateur only. This is about
all I have to say concerning myself individually, and
having said this, I shall now proceed with the DISSERTA-
TION ON THE BANJO, only repeating the request, that the
reader, if he is disposed to ridicule, may reserve his decision in the case in hand until after the trial; or, in other
words, that he will first read the entire work, and then,
*when familiar with the subject*, pass judgment—not
before.

# THE BANJO.

## SECTION I.

"There are more things in heaven and earth than
are dreamed of in your philosophy."—*Shakspeare.*

Who would have thought, a generation ago, that the
Banjo would have ever become the popular and pleasing
instrument it is to-day?

True science derives its conclusions from *facts*, and
facts are said to be *stubborn things*; therefore the cynical
observer may declare that a *mule* is a fact, and perhaps,
according to this logic, he would be correct.

A fact is that which is self evident; that which is often
termed *scientific*, proves frequently, upon investigation,
to be very *unscientific*. In music, art is inter-linked with
science; for music itself is an art, its basis a science.

The so called scientific musician often fails to please—
"to carry his audience with him." People listen, and
there appears to them to have been something lacking.
They have listened to the *science* without the true art; as
some say, "the music lacks soul."

Then whence really comes this power—this art of producing music? If from the brain and nervous system of
man, the scalpel of science has never found it—never
demonstrated it. The mind of man is truly a marvelous
psychic indescribable something, which is far beyond the
reach and grasp of so called science. Music as an art,
is equally as far beyond the reach of the scalpel of the
musical scientist, as is the mind, or as that subtle power

which moves the genius in music, is beyond the scalpel
of the anatomist and physiologist. Genius has evolved
from the crude Banjo a delicate musical instrument,
capable of much power and expression. Science must
step in and endeavor to explain the workings of this
musical instrument, and elucidate its principles. Science
(what is termed science, I mean, not true science) must
ever pale before true art—before genius.

When you hear a person exclaim : " There is no music
whatever in a Banjo," you may know that such person is
neither a scientist nor a philosopher. For many are the
facts which prove that *there is music in a Banjo*. Furthermore, it is a philosophical fact that there is music in the
Banjo, because there are thousands who can testify that
through the avenue of one of the five senses—that of
hearing—they have been made conscious of the fact that
music has been produced. And again, by the exercise
of another of the five senses—that of seeing—they have
been enabled to perceive that the music came from no
other source than a Banjo. They have seen the Banjo—
have listened to its voice, and perhaps have exercised
another of the five senses and felt the Banjo with their
hands. The senses named—seeing, hearing and feeling,
are, I believe, the majority of the senses usually existing
in most persons ; there are, however, some who cannot
hear—some who cannot see. The former we call deaf;
the latter, blind. There are again others who cannot
speak, these we term dumb ; there are a few who cannot
feel—have lost that sense through disease, such as
paralysis. Those deficient in this way could not testify
to such a fact as the Banjo possessing musical powers,
simply because they are through physical deformities or
imperfections rendered incapable.

We find others who are in active possession of all of

the five senses and can hear, can feel, can see; and yet connot hear any music in anything—cannot feel any sympathy for anything — cannot see anything but discord and inaccuracies in the entire universe— or as much of it as they are able to grasp. Some of these are chronic dyspeptics; others live only to get money, and care for nothing else. A few of these would like to have had a hand in the creation of the world; they would have improved upon the work of the Omnipotent.

He who can hear, and hear aright; he who possesses what is called a *musical ear*—he who is by nature capable of perceiving the true grandness and beauties of nature; he who loves to listen to the joyous songs of merry birds, he who sees music and celestial harmony in everything created, is indeed a harmonious and happy individual. He *knows* there is music in the Banjo. Some of my readers upon getting thus far may be tempted to cast the book aside with a sneer, and say, "what nonsense" —"what bosh!" But sneers are not science; neither is the reasoning of such persons philosophic, and consesequently will affect the work little. Nor will the fear of such criticisms change "one jot nor one tittle" of my testimony in this case. I am coming as rapidly as possible to perhaps a more interesting phase of the subject in hand. I assert that the Banjo, as it is constructed to-day—that is, the "Silver-Rim Banjo," is a MUSICAL INSTRUMENT, and as such is as much entitled to respect as the guitar, the harp, the zither, the mandolin, or the piano. This argument I shall endeavor to philosophically sustain. ———

The "Silver-Rim" Banjo, as originally made by Wilson\* and Farnham, in Troy, N. Y., and improved upon

\*See *The Banjo Philosophically*, published by the author, for fuller information.

by the late Jas. W. Clarke, of New York city, and further improved upon by myself and other manufacturers of this day, is conceded to be *the Banjo*—the recognized Banjo of professional and amateur players alike.

This Banjo has a perfect right to the claim of being called a musical instrument. It is constructed upon scientific principles, although these principles may differ materially from those upon which the construction of the guitar or harp are based. Briefly speaking, I may describe it as follows : Its body consists of a circular frame which is termed the rim. This rim is composed of metal and wood, used in combination, as it were.

The metal used is the alloy commonly called German silver, which is also nickel-plated, and its polished surface presents an attractive appearance. On the inside of the metal rim is found the rim of wood ; the wood rim and metal rim being so made and united as to form one rim.

Over this rim is stretched—tightly stretched—the head which is made of calf skin and may be called the sound-ing-board of the instrument. A system of brackets, screws and nuts present an attractive appearance ; and with their aid we are enabled to stretch the head and always have it tense and firm. This is accomplished by having a narrow band or hoop, made very strong, neatly fit over the head which is tucked around a wire ring ; and the hooks or screws, drawing upon this hoop, strain the head and hold it evenly in place.

Fitted to this rim is a neck, made of suitable wood, such as cherry, maple, walnut or rosewood, which must be accurately adjusted. The upper surface of this neck is called the *fingerboard*, and is veneered or covered with ebony, or other hard wood, to render it more durable, and also to give the neck greater strength, and cause it to resist the tension of the strings ; for the strings with

which the instrument is strung, and which are vibrated to
produce the musical tones, pass over this fingerboard, or
face of the neck.  The strings, five in number,* are
stretched from the little appendage known as the tail-
piece, over the surface of the head, four of them extending to the extreme end of the neck or fingerboard, to the
scroll or "screw-head," where they are twisted around
suitable pegs, by the turning of which the tension of the
strings may be altered, and their pitch raised or lowered.
The remaining string, called the fifth, or thumb-string,
does not extend over the entire length of the fingerboard,
but only about, generally speaking, two-thirds the distance, where a peg is fitted in the side of the neck to
receive it.  The strings pass over a bridge, which is made
of maple wood, generally, and rests upon the surface of
the head, in a manner similiar to the bridge of a violin.
The bridge conducts the vibrations of the strings to the
membraneous head, which is elastic, and acts as a sound
board.

The "fifth string" of the Banjo is said to have been
added to the instrument by one Joe Sweeney of Virginia,†
several years ago ; but whether this is true or not, I have
no personal knowledge nor reliable information.  But it
is a fact nevertheless, that the fifth string has "stuck to"
the Banjo, and a Banjo to-day would not be a Banjo
without its short fifth, or thumb string, "octave string,"
or "little E," as some call it.   And, although at various
times players have made moves to do away with this
string ; such movements have not met with success, nor
do I believe that they ever will.   For it is this little string

---

*The American Banjo is strung with five strings generally;
but occasionally an additional Bass string is added.   The English Banjo is strung with six and seven strings.

†See The Banjo Philosophically.

which gives to the Banjo its "ring," and which com-
pletes the octave in tuning the four gut strings; and in
short, makes the Banjo a Banjo.

---

The strings of the Banjo produce five notes only when
played in their natural position, or "open." But by the
use of the fingerboard, using the fingers of the left hand
to "stop" the string—that is, to press them to the finger-
board, thus shortening their vibrating length, in a similar
manner to those of the violin or guitar; we are enabled
to produce on the five strings, but mainly upon four, all
the notes of the chromatic scale within a compass of
about three octaves. And the quality of the music produced by the manipulation of these three octaves of
notes, depends of course, upon the skill of the player
and upon the musical qualities of his particular Banjo.
It does not follow, by any manner of means, that because
many Banjos have a similar appearance, or are presum-
ably constructed in one way, that their musical qualities
will be the same; for this is not the case, as I shall explain before I am done with the subject.

---

When the strings of the Banjo are caused to vibrate;
the vibration, through the medium of the bridge, is conducted to the head; and the head being in itself an
elastic sonorous body and tightly strained over the rim,
as has been said, conducts the vibration thereto. All
vibration produces *sound waves*—motion in the air; un-
seen, but audible to the ear. The strings alone, not only
of the Banjo, but of any musical instrument, produce
little volume of tone in themselves—the sound waves
produced by a string vibrating alone in the air, and not

conducted to any sonorous body—giving an almost inaudible sound.

This is a fact with which nearly every school boy is familiar, and is demonstrated so readily that little need be said regarding it.

The head of the Banjo, as I have said, is elastic. It is a sonorous body in itself. Where could you find a drum that would produce sound without it? The head then acts as a sounding-board; the strings produce vibration; this vibration is transmitted to the head; the head also, to a certain extent, vibrates—although on a different principle from the strings—for stretched strings vibrate in an oscillating movement between their fixed ends; whilst the head is stretched in the form of a circle, (the emblem of Creation) and has no ends; but is firmly fixed all round.

The vibrations of the head are conducted to the circular frame over which it is stretched, and although the head is perhaps the most important factor in the acoustical construction of the Banjo, it is useless alone—equally as useless as the strings, if used alone. As no one good action in life constitutes a perfect man; no one properly constructed *part* of a musical instrument constitutes a perfect instrument in the whole. All its parts have a bearing upon the whole. It is therefore of the highest importance that the rim structure of the instrument be made to harmonize with the head and strings in giving forth vibration, or musical sound. The head and rim being, as it were, united and parts of one whole, so far as mechanical construction is concerned; must likewise be united in affinity, so as to act as one in producing the necessary vibration. If this is not accomplished, we have an instrument, which, like "a house divided against itself," cannot stand. Now the vibration of the strings being conducted to the head by means of the bridge, and again to the rim by the means of the head, it follows that the rim should be so constituted as to respond to, and as far as possible mingle its vibration with that of the head and strings. The rim then, being the body and structure of the Banjo, is not far from being the most important part of its structure, and the most difficult part to make properly. The neck deserves also much consideration ; for no matter how well the head is stretched, and how perfect the rim may be, if the neck is not properly made and properly adjusted to the rim, it is impossible to perform upon the instrument with accuracy or with any degree of satisfaction.

The sounding quality of any substance depends upon its hardness and elasticity. The rim must be sufficiently elastic for its purpose and yet of sufficient hardness or strength to remain firm and withstand the strain of the head.

The head must also be firm and elastic. A firm strong head without sufficient elasticity is useless ; and one that is too elastic, and lacking firmness, is likewise useless. It is therefore necessary to secure these two important factors in the banjo head—firmness (or strength) and elasticity.

Now, when the head is damp or wet, it becomes, as it were, slack, and is then too elastic for producing a good musical tone, and that which is most desired in a Banjo is a bright, clear (or sharp) musical tone, with sufficient power to fill a good sized room or hall.

This "sharp" tone in the Banjo mainly depends ; Upon the tension of the strings.

Upon the musical quality, size, tension and elasticity of the head.

Upon the size, weight and sonorous qualities of the rim.

And also upon, in a great measure, the length of the neck (because of tension and length of vibrating strings).

A loose, flabby head is much like a loose flabby string, in producing vibration. A head that is damp, or loose and flabby, will not have sufficient tension upon the rim to cause it to properly respond to its vibrations; neither are the vibrations of such a head rapid enough to produce what is called a "sharp tone." It is similar to a string which is loosely stretched and therefore produces a slow vibration and consequently a low tone—only that the musical *pitch* of the instrument entirely depends upon the strings—the musical quality of that pitch upon the tension of the head, etc.

The neck of the Banjo, at first sight, appears to be a very simple part to construct, but this is quite far from being the real case; for to make an instrument with a neck that will perfectly retain its shape and not warp or change with the varying climate, and will withstand the manipulation of the pegs with all the various changes in tension, produced by various pitches in tuning and strings of various degrees of thickness is a matter which requires considerable skill and practical experience.

———

I have heard the remark passed by certain persons, whose knowledge of the subject was exceedingly limited, that the Banjo could not be a musical instrument because it was open inside—had no back—was not closed in, like the guitar or violin. The reasoning of such persons I hold to be very fallacious. Might as well assert that the xylophone should not be used in an orchestra because it is only constructed of solid blocks of wood placed upon straw or cords. A flute is a musical instrument; yet it is constructed upon a different principle from a violin. You may reply that one is a wind instrument whilst the other is a stringed instrument, and there can therefore be no comparison between them. This I grant. But I likewise assert that two stringed instruments may be constructed upon different principles, so far as their sounding bodies are concerned, and yet have an equally just claim to being called musical instruments.

Comparing, for instance, the Banjo with the guitar, I would briefly say: The quality of the Banjo's tone is brilliant and enlivening, while that of the guitar is soft and soothing—more subdued than that of the Banjo. Now, how are they different; why are they so different in quality?

The guitar has a back to it; it is closed in with the exception of the "sound-hole." In this enclosure there is an air body. Nothing is empty—"Nature abhors a vacuum,"—therefore the inside of the guitar is filled with air. Now, when its strings are put in vibration, the agitation produced by this vibration compresses the air body within the instrument, and this air body instantly expands and the sound waves are sent forth.

The top of the guitar is constructed of soft wood; the back of harder wood. The air body within is connected directly with the air without by means of the sound-hole in the top. The character of the tone of this instrument then depends:

Upon its size and shape, and consequently upon the air-body within, its specific density and quantity or size.

Upon its strings—their tension and thickness.

Upon the bridge over which the strings pass.

Upon the sonorous qualities of the wood used in the construction of its top sides and back; and upon their thickness.

And finally, upon the perfect fitting and adjustment of all the parts and their harmonious blending and affinity.

The Banjo, as I have previously explained, has no air body within it that is enclosed, so to speak, and which sends forth sound-waves from a hole called the sound-hole, like the guitar, and its principle is therefore somewhat different from the guitar, as I have previously explained.

Not many years ago there was a Banjo gotten up and said to have been patented, called the "closed back Banjo." This instrument was evidently placed upon the market with the idea of supplying the demand for a Banjo that was not a Banjo, but was an attempt at something else—purely a miscarriage of ideas. People did not understand the Banjo very well then, and one of the chief objections of musicians to the instrument was that it was *too open*, and therefore must give forth a hollow, flat sound.

If I remember rightly, the manufacturer of this particular Banjo, which for a time had a large sale, although I seldom find one of them in use now (proving that they were not as good as others), claimed that the Banjo was the only instrument made which was open in the back, and from which *all the tone proceeded from the back*, and consequently must either come out from behind the performer or else he must turn his back to his audience so that the tone should go directly to them, and not be swallowed up in the scenery of the theatre or by the screens, as the case may have been. To obviate this, and cause the tone to go directly out in front of the

player, he constructed a peculiar kind of narrow rim and
boxed it in all round, leaving an inch or so margin for
the tone to come out; which it was supposed to do, after
going through the head and striking against the back,
something like a ball thrown against the side of a house.
But as sound-waves do not exactly act upon the principle
of a bouncing ball, the closed back Banjo was not a
success. It was loud, but the loudness was caused rather
by compound and conflicting vibrations than by increased musical power of tone, and had therefore a certain lack of musical quality and carrying power, and
therefore the Banjo of that character was soon tabooed
by the Banjo-playing public—plenty of them soon being
found for sale in pawnbrokers' establishments. The
manufacturer, I understand, disposed of his patent, and
a music firm lost money in it.

After the patent had been disposed of, the inventor lost
no time in placing upon the market a "patent open-back"
Banjo, constructed upon another principle, but equally
as crude and fallacious as the "closed back" Banjo.

Such manufacturers being ignorant of the first principles of acoustics ; or what is still worse, caring only to
get money from an easily deceived and gullible public ;
are not the ones to lend a helping hand towards evolving
and developing the higher possibilities of the Banjo as a
musical instrument.

---

Banjos constructed with rims of solid metal, such as
bell metal rims, for instance, have been made with the
erroneous supposition that the natural "ring" of the
metal would be added to the vibrations of the head and
strings and cause a clear, bell-like tone. Such ideas have
been worked upon by persons not sufficiently acquainted
with musical or acoustical laws to guide them in their

experiments, and by others who cared not what kind of a Banjo was manufactured so long as they could call it a "patent banjo," and give it an attractive name, so as to catch the eye and ear. Hence, such melodious titles as "Bell Rim Banjo," "Patent Bell Banjo," etc., have been used to advertise Banjos which were at best second or third rate instruments.

To construct an instrument with a legitimate *bell rim* that would add its tone to the vibration of the strings, is not in accordance with any known law of acoustics. This I have explained fully in my former publication, previously alluded to, *The Banjo Philosophically*. A bell fixed in any way in the rim of a Banjo would add. only to the tone of such notes or chords as were in harmony with the natural tone of the bell. And hence, were a Banjo so constructed that a bell was placed within or connected to it, and the strings tuned in unison (or in harmony) with the tone of the bell; the "open string" notes of the instrument might be greatly louder and more bell-like than without the bell; but when played upon in different positions and chords—chords which were not in harmony with the bell—the volume of tone would not be in any way augmented by reason of the bell.

Persons unfamiliar with music and unacquainted with natural philosophy, are the ones who purchase such Banjos; led on by the tempting sound of the name and unfamiliar with the tone of a Banjo. Experienced performers, who have had their "eye teeth cut," do not purchase such instruments; and the manufacturers of them must in time, and at no far distant day, be made familiar with the "Hand writing on the Wall"—their Kingdom numbered and finished.

No one can censure those who have been compelled to listen to the music produced from improperly constructed Banjos in the hands of unskilled players, for saying that " there is no music in a Banjo." No one can blame those who have never heard the violin played by a master—never heard it except as a harsh toned fiddle in the hands of a country dance scraper—for declaring that " a fiddle is the devil of an instrument." For there are violins that talk when the master plays them, and there are violins that squawk when the fiddler scrapes them. And there are Banjos that speak when an artist bids them, and Banjos that merely " plunk " when an unskilled performer handles them.

## SECTION II.

"The thing (Banjo) has no musical merit whatever."
*Unknown Musical Bigot.*

"It is claimed by those competent to judge, that the Banjo will some day rival the violin as a solo instrument, and it is a fact that the most cultured people of Europe and America have taken up the Banjo, and find in its study the most delightful recreation."—*N. Y. Herald.*

"The concert made quite a new departure in Banjo playing, and proved that the instrument can be used with advantage in many combinations suited to the concert-hall."—*Boston Herald.*

You have all heard of Paganini, whose name stands immortal and at the front rank of violinists. He was an Italian. In Gardiner's *Music of Nature* will be found an account of the marvelous sensation created by him in London in the year 1831. Later on I shall have something to say about a similar sensation created by an American Banjo player, E. M. Hall, in London, in the year 1880—fifty-one years later.

Musical and other encyclopædias, dictionaries and musical works give a very vague and meagre account of the Banjo. Who can blame them ? The majority of such works in use to-day were published years ago; or at least the matter contained within their covers was written several years back. Webster states, in his dictionary, that the name, at least, "Banjo," is not of negro origin, but was corrupted from *bandore*, which is an instrument of the guitar species. It matters little how it was named or from whence the name came—the name has a

musical sound, is short and easy to remember : It therefore answers the purpose. The statement contained in
Stainer and Barretts' *Dictionary of Musical Terms*, that
the Banjo is one of the most important musical instruments employed by minstrel troupes, is also incorrect, so
far as the present day and generation is concerned ; for
many prominent ministrel companies employ no Banjo
player at all. I have myself been present at such entertainments where there was no Banjo used, and the leading instruments were the usual orchestral instruments—
violin, flutes, horns, etc. The statements published in
other books of like character, that the Banjo is very
limited in capability and only fit for simple times and
accompaniments, is likewise incorrect when applied to
the Banjo of the day (the properly constructed Banjo.)
This I have dwelt upon at greater length in different
issues of the *Banjo and Guitar Journal*, published by
myself, which articles have doubtless been perused by
many of my readers.

But, as I said before, these works are old, and applied,
if they ever applied at all, to the early Banjo, and their
statements are of slight import to the Banjo players of
this generation, unless it is to show them what their
favorite instrument was, some years ago, in a past generation.

Other encyclopædias will be published—new dictionaries must be compiled and printed to meet the requirements of an advancing civilization. Let us hope that
when such books appear they will contain a better account of an instrument which America claims as her
own, and of which Americans have just cause to be
proud.

A few years backward I gaze and I see in this dim past
that the Banjo was going along smoothly, making time at

a fair gait—making itself known, attracting admirers and among a large class of people gaining adherents. Thalberg, the well-known pianist, is said to have been infatuated with it, and to have become a player upon it. Books were published which began to give it a firmer footing. But, then, suddenly a dark cloud seemed to hover over it, shadowing its very existence. It was not unlike that great, black-winged creature, the Raven, written of by a gifted poet, which—

> "Perched upon a bust of Pallas,
> Just above my chamber-door."

Seemed to say, "I will haunt you until I blacken your very existence, and I will not leave you until I have so shaken you that you will never—no, never, recover from the effects of my presence."

This polluted creature appeared in the shape of a "catch-penny" system of learning to play the banjo, called by its projectors the "*simplified method.*" It was without method or system. It had not the slightest foundation to stand upon; therefore was it called the *simplified*, or *simple*, method.

It was so simple in its construction that musicians called it rightly named: *a simple method for the simple-minded*, and just the thing for such a miserable instrument as the Banjo. It was so easy and so simple a system of learning to play, that a person could, with the aid of one of its books, which cost all the way from one dollar to five dollars each, learn to pick out, with perhaps one finger and thumb, on the Banjo strings, such soul inspiring tunes as "Sho-fly, don't bodder me," "Carry me back to Ole Virginny," etc. The flies surely would cease to bother such manipulators of such tunes and also doubtless wish that some well-disposed person would indeed carry them (or the method) back to Old

Virginny. The students of this method rarely ever got any further. They had taken the express train for Banjo Botchtown; the journey was short, and few got any further. Some lived to return and start over again by another route, but their number was few indeed, and of the weak ones who had once partaken of a dose of the "method," many fainted by the wayside after starting upon the right track.

All this means, reader, that a set of unscruplous individuals, possessing a very limited knowledge of music, and very little love for the science or art,—and therefore being ignorant and also disinclined to labor or effort—did not feel inclined to spend their valuable time in teaching pupils to play the Banjo properly. It was too hard work and did not agree with them. Besides, many who would gladly pay money to know how to play the Banjo, would not pay money for being taught a lot of rubbish about notes, rests, bars, etc. They wanted to learn to manipulate the strings "right off," without any waste of time. It was also frequently very difficult for these professors of the Banjo to instruct pupils in musical notation, for the reason that they themselves knew so very little about it; and pupils often had a habit of asking very troublesome questions about chords, time, &c., which made it quite unpleasant for the teacher, who did not want to be bothered. What he wanted most and only, was to secure a good fee for a " quarters' lessons " in advance and then let the pupils come in when he was out; or what was nearly as bad—come in and sit down to a beer drinking bout; picking on the Banjo at the same time, or between whiles.

Hence, a system by which a person could learn to pick a few tunes on the Banjo *without study*, and without having to "learn music," was in demand. If such a thing could be gotten up, there was money in the scheme; it would sell well all over the country. This accounts for the origination of the so-called easy system, or simplified method. An ignorant pupil could not understand why the five lines of the musical stave should not represent the *five strings of the Banjo*. Demand caused supply; the five lines were made to represent five strings. An open string was noted as a round o (whole note). A stopped note was represented by a black note. This was termed the "open and closed note" method. Knowing ones dubbed it the "open and shut" method; which name still clings to it. It added greatly to ignorance, by closing for a time the door of knowledge. It never made one good player. It opened the door to ignorance, and it put back the Banjo for some time. It was a system that was not a system—a method that had no method whatever in it. It served its purpose; made money for its instigators and enabled many ignoramuses to set up as teachers,—teaching how *not* to become a Banjo player.

---

But there is no cloud, however dark, that has not a silver lining; and darkness in this case soon began to give place to light.

Gradually the star arose and the light brightened, and

> "Through the gates of amethyst and amber
> Shined the kindling glories of the morning."

To you reader,—to perhaps whom poetical language is a stranger, and liable to be misunderstood—I will speak in plainer words. I mean that as the powers of darkness were working to consume the very vitals of the Banjo, the powers of light were at the same time at work—working to elevate and raise it. The force of the "simplified method" systems having done so much to *pull down*, in

the minds of intelligent people, caused a limited number
of ardent lovers of the instrument to set to work more
vigorously to elevate and to *build up*.   Thus it is that
suitable books and sheet music publications were produced to gradually take the place of the worthless " easy
methods."   Those who had forsaken the instrument on
account of not being able to obtain suitable music, began
to renew their interest in it.    Intelligent people and musicians, seeing musical works in good form for the Banjo,
were compelled to notice it.   Gradually it took upon itself
renewed life.   So that at the present time we have many
good instruction books for the Banjo, and a great number of pieces of music, of various degrees of difficulty;
which stock is being constantly added to ; and although
there is still some demand from a certain class of persons, for "tunes" written by the " simple method," yet
the percentage of such demand is small in comparison to
the constantly increasing demand for music (legitimate
music) of a good character ; and through the publication
of good music, properly written and adapted to the instrument ; and through a good class of Banjo books and
literature, is the instrument to be finally raised to its
proper place and position as a musical instrument.

## THE REQUIREMENTS OF A "SOLO BANJO."

A Banjo to be used for an instrumental performance,
or for playing solos with piano accompaniment, must
possess the following characteristics :—

Acuteness of tone, intensity, resonance.
Musical purity, carrying power.
Free vibration.
Easy action.

Harmonious action, equalization of upper and lower registers.

Such a Banjo must possess a *musical tone;* for indeed there can be no carrying power without it, and, at the same time, the Banjo characteristic of the tone must not be relinquished nor its individuality lost.

This desideratum has not been accomplished by "closing the back," nor by what has been called the Patent Bell-rim Banjo, etc. For proof of this you have only to look about you and see that such Banjos are not used by players of note, and that professional players, as a rule, use entirely the *Silver Rim Banjo*, as I have previously stated.

Whilst it is not impossible to construct a good instrument without metal in the rim, it is yet exceedingly rare to find one so constructed that meets the requirements of a good player. And whilst I do not assert that only *"silver rim"* Banjos can be good, I do most emphatically say that the *silver rim Banjo* is, and has been for years past, the *model Banjo*, and the Banjo used by the best players.

It is not altogether impossible that a Banjo can be constructed, having a closed back and sides, that will make good music—nor do I say that this has never been accomplished; but at the same time, any school-boy of average intelligence can see that such an instrument must be constructed upon, and must be governed by other principles than those found in the silver rim open-back Banjo. It is also possible that a Banjo may be constructed with a "bell," so that such a bell would act directly upon the tone of the open strings and thus make such a Banjo suitable to use for a "swinging act," or the "Bell Chimes" imitation; but such a Banjo would be useful for nothing else, and I am of the opinion that the silver rim Banjo, when properly constructed, possesses all the requirements needed for any and every kind of Banjo-playing.

## SECTION III.

"Music hath charms to soothe the savage breast."

"If I were de President ob dese United States,
I'd lick molasses candy and swing upon de gates."

*Jim Crow.*

THE ideal of the undeveloped and crude mind (if such mind can be said to have an ideal) is far different from that of the more advanced student and thinker. Thus the lines sung by the darkey in the past generation, expressing his highest ambition, and telling us what he would do were he the President of the United States, convey to us the idea that licking molasses candy and swinging upon gates were about the highest conceptions old Jim could form of the duties and requirements of the highest office attainable by any American citizen.

Some of the conceptions of people (and people who are old enough, big enough, and should be wise enough to know better) of the present day, concerning the Banjo and the Banjo-player, are equally as crude as the conceptions of the negro regarding the presidency.

I have met those who thought that the Banjo was a tambourine with a neck in it, and that the rim was to be jingled against the sides when played, in the fashion of a "tom-tom," for instance. I have met others who thought that because a man was a Banjo-player, that he should never get tired of *playing*—should play in the morning, play at noon, and play again in the evening, and continue to play as the evening continued into night and night rolled around the circle to dawn. Such people must be taught better—those who will not feel for others should be made to feel.

Many beginners on the Banjo have no intention of making a *study* of the instrument. They take it up for recreation, and their ideas concerning it being at the beginning undeveloped, they like only simple tunes, such as are whistled by the boys in the streets; the ear capable of distinguishing *harmony* not yet being sufficiently developed. As such pupils advance, many of them desire to learn more of the instrument, and with each step of advancement comes further desire to progress. From step to step, then, the Banjo-player is made.

Nothing is accomplished all at once; little by little, knowledge of any kind is attained. A man cannot become a musician in a day, in a week, nor in a month. And yet this fact should deter no one—and will not deter anyone possessing average intelligence and pluck—from seeking to gain a knowledge of music and of Banjo playing. When once obtained, such knowledge can never be entirely lost; and even should the Banjo be laid aside and all musical exercise be suspended for months or years, should the person again take it up, he has a good foundation upon which to begin again.

It is a mistaken idea with many persons that one may acquire a knowledge of the Banjo or other instruments "by ear," and without a proper course of musical studies. I have, in my experience, met with very few really good performers upon the Banjo or guitar who had not, at some time or other, studied the rudiments of music. Here and there, but very occasionally, I have met with a really good Banjo-player who seemed to possess no knowledge whatever of musical notation; but it has invariably been the case that such performers have been associated for years with capable musicians, and with the possession of a very fine musical ear, have been enabled to develop a sense of hearing and a comprehension o musical sounds and chords which enabled them to readily perform very difficult music. But it must be understood that such players have had the advantages of the constant association of musicians who were often adepts at musical science, so to speak, and who therefore possessed theoretical and practical knowledge of music in all its forms ; so that really those ear players, so-called, who played so well "by ear," had been compelled to spend a large portion of their time in studying in their own peculiar way, all that they played. Such a performer could perhaps play a certain piece after having heard it a few times, passably well, or exceedingly well, as the case may have been ; but an ordinary player, possessing the average knowledge of musical notation, could have played the same piece in the same manner, directly from the notes, not requiring to hear the piece played at all, and the same amount of time spent in training the ear to imitate, and the fingers to manipulate the strings that is necessitated in learning to play well "by ear," if spent in learning to play from music would place the performer in possession of valuable knowledge as well as develop his musical skill, and he would be something better than a mere parrot-like performer, who must first hear, or have played for him, everything he learns. Not only this, but it is a fact that very few of the small number of "ear players" upon either the guitar or Banjo, peform accurately. Even when they attain to the correct rendition of a musical composition, they soon forget, after not having played or heard it for a time, and then render it more and more inaccurately, or so changed and intermingled with passages of their own as to become sometimes unrecognizable to the musician who composed it. But with the majority of players upon any instrument who possess no theoretical musical knowledge, it is found

that they do not play any musical composition entirely
correct, nor as the composer intended. It is true that
with many of them conceit is so closely interwoven with
ignorance that they suppose they are playing with great
skill and musical effect, and where their audiences are of
a musically-ignorant class, their performances please and
are accounted sometimes wonderful. But when learned
musicians chance to hear them play, they are at once
made familiar with the fact that they are listening to an
"ear-player," and not to a musician. A certain amount
of musical knowledge can hurt no one, and it is better
for all who attempt to learn to perform upon any instrument, whether it be Banjo, guitar, or what not; to place
themselves under the instruction of a competent music-
teacher, or at least possess themselves of suitable books
of instruction, and devote a portion of their spare time
daily to studying them. It may be said, "I have no
spare time." I reply—every one has spare time. He
who has the most to do often finds time for doing things
that others who have nothing whatever to do but to eat,
drink, sleep, dress and yawn, could not possibly spare the
time to accomplish. A great deal of time is wasted during the day or week which might be well spent in going
through a book, *a little at a time*. The little drops fill
the bucket and the little grains of sand make up the sea-
shore.

Do not be content to follow those who say, "Let us
eat, drink and be merry, for to-morrow we die." Nothing
is accomplished without effort — nothing, absolutely
nothing. No goal is reached—no journey ended, without
a move; sitting still will not take you there. Had I sat
down and waited for the Banjo to become a popular and
recognized instrument, I should have had to wait so long
that the time would never have come. I'm waiting yet,

perhaps, but I'm also *working* to bring about and to accomplish what I desire. Any rock can be moved if you have only a fulcrum and a sufficiently long lever. The rock I am moving is the people—musical people; my lever and fulcrum are *work* and *perseverance*. You, too, must take hold and help, and before long the musical tones of the Banjo will ring in the homes of the people—in the happy homes and light hearts of many—all over the land.

## ON BANJO PLAYING.

In order to fully comprehend, the mind must be superior in development to the thing comprehended. I have met frequently, in my experience with persons who possesssed no knowledge of music, were what is called "ear-players" on the Banjo, and who really believed that they could correctly accompany any piece of music or song after once hearing it. To call attention to the mistakes made by such players is often purely a waste of time; for they cannot see that they are not finished performers, or that their chords are often incorrect. There is an old saying—"Never argue with an ignorant man." It is simply a waste of time and nerve force to do so in most instances. Whilst I heartily recommend the reader to lend his aid and assistance to anyone who is endeavoring to learn; I cannot advise anyone to attempt to *force* knowledge, or his individual opinions, upon anyone whatever, for—

> "He who's convinced against his will,
> Is of the same opinion still."

Now, having advised the Banjoist in all cases to acquire a knowledge of his instrument philosophically, I am called upon to throw out some hints that will be of service to him in this direction. Some suggestions which are the result of my own practical experience and extended observation may therefore not be out of place; although this present work is by no means to be considered a Banjo Instructor. My former books, comprising such well-known instructors as the *Complete American Banjo School, Thorough School for the Banjo*, etc., being all that is considered necessary, so far as learning to play the instrument properly, by note, is concerned. Yet there are other matters than notes and chords to be considered in acquiring a proper knowledge of Banjo-playing, and a portion of my lecture, *The Banjo Philosophically*, bearing upon this branch of the subject, having met with so much favor, I feel that a little further said upon the same subject may not be amiss. Of course, practical experience is the best, and sometimes the only teacher in many things, but no one can learn music properly from experience alone. Such an undertaking would require the time of many human existences. It is therefore necessary that there should be a ground-work, or foundation, to start from, and a certain set of rules, so to speak, from which to work.

It is true that "practice makes perfect." It is likewise true that "knowledge is the guide of practice," and without this knowledge one is often compelled to grope along in the dark, often wasting all his energies in misdirected effort.

"Lost motion" in machinery is avoided. So should lost energy be avoided in study and practice when possible. He who is rightly guided and directed, all things being equal, must reach his goal sooner than he who through misdirected effort is compelled to "begin over again" many times. The man who goes to sea with a compass and understands navigation, is almost sure to

reach port before the man who goes to sea without a
compass and who does not understand navigation,—if he
is ever fortunate enough to reach it at all. There are, of
course, those who will not accept any suggestions from
another. These are to be met with almost daily and in
every known business and profession. These I will leave
to themselves.

There are others who never care to rely upon themselves at all, but are ready always to follow the advice of
others, however unreliable and unworthy such advice
may be. To these I say, learn to think; weigh what is
given as advice; learn to think for yourselves; "*Prove
all things; hold fast to that which is good.*" I do not
set myself up as an infallible teacher of music or the art
of Banjo-playing, and as I have said in *The Banjo
Philosophically*, I do not expect to hold the same opinion
one day that I hold another. "A wise man changes his
opinion; a fool, never." I have ever sought to learn
everything that pertains to my business. To accomplish this I must necessarily progress; and in progressing,
when observation and experience teach me that I have
been wrong in any preconceived opinion, I hope that I
shall at least be manly enough to acknowledge it and
relinquish it for a better.

Such being my views, I cannot ask anyone to blindly
relinquish their own opinions and customs for those
which I may offer or suggest in their place. I aim simply
to suggest what seems to me to be proper—nothing
further. I desire no one to say at any time, " I did so
and so because Stewart recommended it;" or " I have
changed my Banjo because Stewart said in his book that
it was not the kind for me to use."

The same liberty of action I demand for myself, I am
ever willing that others should enjoy. More than this,

I am ever ready and willing to receive any suggestions which my readers may see fit to make that are of interest to the rising school of Banjo-players. With these brief remarks I will now proceed with the subject in hand.

---

There are two separate and distinct styles of Banjo-playing taught in the various books and schools of instruction. One is the old style—original style—called "stroke playing;" the other is the more finished and established style of the day, originally copied from the guitar, and therefore called guitar style, or "picking." There are few good players of the stroke style. There are many good players of the other style.

In the stroke style the first finger and thumb of the right hand only are used to manipulate the strings, which are struck downwards with the finger and plucked with the thumb. The finger is covered with a "thimble,"

made of light and elastic metal. This thimble serves to strike the string a clear sharp blow, and the tone produced, so far as music is concerned, depends upon the skill of the performer.

Anyone can draw a violin bow over the strings of a violin and produce a harsh, rasping sound; but it lies with the *artist* to use the bow in such a manner as to produce clear musical tones. The Banjo thimble acts in almost the same way. Almost anyone can put on a thimble and pound on the strings of the Banjo; but to produce a musical tone and execute rapid and brilliant

passages, is a matter not so easy, and one which is accomplished only with the aid of proper instruction in the beginning, and continued, persevering practice afterwards.
A few points on thimble playing, together with exercises
for practice, are to be found in the *Complete American
Banjo School*, part first, which may be had of the author
or through responsible music dealers.

In the guitar style of Banjo-playing—which is the
proper style to acquire first, at any rate; the little finger
of the right hand is rested upon the head, near the bridge;
the bridge commonly used being of the size and appearance of the diagram here given:

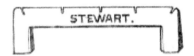

The little finger resting upon the head* serves as a rest
to the hand and a resistance to the movement of picking
the strings, without which it is difficult to execute rapid
or brilliant staccato passages.   The forearm rests lightly
upon the rim.

In the beginning it is best to acquire a knowledge of
picking the strings with the use of the first and second
fingers and thumb only, allowing the third finger to remain idle until the other fingers have become thoroughly
accustomed to their work.   Indeed, there are many brilliant pieces which may readily be executed with the two
fingers and thumb as well as with three—and this is the
case to such an extent that experienced players are called

---

* Some few performers play without the aid of the rest afforded
by the little finger resting upon the head, but a good execution
among such is unusual.   Chords, however, may as readily be
played in that manner with practice.

upon to exercise judgment as to the proper method of handling any particular composition. The three fingers are almost invariably used in playing chords and accompaniments to songs, &c.

There is a movement in Banjo-playing which is called the *tremolo*. This is the most beautiful and effective movement of which the instrument is capable. Some melodies may be played in tremolo upon the first string of the instrument and at the same time an accompaniment played to the melody, upon the remaining strings, rendering a beautiful effect. It was this movement, used in connection with variations upon the melody of *Home, Sweet Home*, which so took the audience by storm when E. M. Hall made his debut in England, in the year 1880.

The tremolo movement is executed with the first finger, oscillating over the string very rapidly, and causing a continuous trill, not unlike the movement of the plectrum upon the strings of the mandolin, only the tone produced is not so harsh and wirey. The hand being free and not compelled to hold a plectrum between the thumb and finger, allows the thumb to act upon the strings not in use for the tremolo, and permits the performer to manipulate the strings so as to play an accompaniment with the thumb, whilst the first finger is producing the tremolo. It is customary to rest the second finger upon the head, in tremolo playing, instead of the little finger, and to manipulate the strings somewhat further from the bridge, which renders the tone softer; the strings being more flexible than very near the bridge.

Most beautiful music may be produced from a good Banjo, properly regulated and strung, and in the hands of a good player, by the tremolo movement. It is capable of exquisite expression. But the movement alone, however expressive it may be, is not nearly so entrancing when used alone as when used in connection with other movements. The various movements, slow and rapid, must be harmonized in the variations on a musical theme, in order to produce the very best effects. The artist in music studies this, as does the painter—the artist in colors. He knows that no one color alone produces a beautiful painting; the colors must be used discriminately; they must be harmoniously blended. And here is where science stops, and true art or genius begins. What rules can teach the blending of colors, so that *any person* can set to work and produce paintings possessing all the artistic merit of the Old Italian Masters ?

Where are the rules by which the ordinary individual can acquire the power of handling the violin as did Paganini ? Here again is where science becomes lost, and unless the individual has within himself that which may be termed a gift, he can get " just so far and no further." Then I say, that although rules are of the highest importance in learning to play upon the Banjo, and although a ground-work in the rudiments of music is almost absolutely essential, yet no amount of study will make a musical artist, or musical expert, of a man who has not music within himself. If the individual " has it in him," he will, by study and practice, step by step, mount the ladder.

I think I hear some one say : " How shall I know whether I have the talent to become a banjoist—a good one?" I reply ; you, yourself perhaps know better than anyone can tell you, whether you have or have not the ability to acquire that which you desire. At all events, you can *try*. Nothing, worth having, is acquired without some effort.

The question may be asked—if resting the end of the finger upon the head does not interfere with the vibration. I reply that to the best of my knowledge it does not materially interfere with the tone of the instrument in any way. I have made experiments in this with several players of ability and known reputation, and the conclusion arrived at has been that the rest of the finger was essential to a brilliant execution—the tone produced being augmented by the rest, from the fact of thus acquiring a more vigorous and sure pluck of the strings.

## TUNING THE BANJO TO ACCORD WITH THE PIANO.

The musical notation of the Banjo is not expressed in the actual key in which the instrument sounds. This has been a puzzling matter to some young players when first attempting to tune their Banjos in accord with the piano. The key noted as A on the Banjo sounds in accord with the key of C on the piano. That is, in the Banjos of ordinary dimensions, and when the piano stands at "concert pitch." Hence all piano accompaniments intended to be used with Banjo solos are written a *minor third* higher than the key in which the Banjo music is noted. Extra large Banjos are generally tuned a full tone lower, and their A is then B flat.

The fact that A on the Banjo is really C on the piano has led some few inexperienced and untutored professors to declare its notation incorrect. This, hower, is not true; for any key may have been used as a basis from which to write music for the instrument, and any of the keys would have answered equally as well to him who was thoroughly accustomed to it. To have called A, C on the Banjo; that is, to have begun its scale in C., instead of A would have had the disadvantage of a large number of ledger lines used above the staff and but one line below, and the only real advantage such notation would have had is that the pupil would naturally have been taught his rudimentary tunes and chords without the use of the signature with its three and four sharps, which often puzzles the beginner.

As to the key in which the Banjo music is written being different from the key in which the piano accompaniment is noted, is of no practical importance, save that it would be more simple and easy for the arranger of the music.

Many of our established orchestral instruments, such as the cornet, clarionet, etc., are noted in a different key from their actual pitch.

Were the logic of some professors of the Banjo to hold good, there would have to be a different notation for every different size of Banjo, exactly in accordance with its musical pitch. This would be sheer nonsense.

Even were the Banjo tuned, played and noted in the "key of C," it would nevertheless be a fact that its notation would still be wrong were we accept the theories and arguments of some of our London "American Banjo Tutors;" for at best the instrument would sound a full octave lower than its notes indicated. The guitar, for instance, is noted in the treble cleff, but sounds its tones in the bass cleff, an octave lower than written.

In tuning the ordinary Banjo with the piano, so as to play the music generally published for these instruments in combination; the strings of the Banjo must accord with the following notes on the piano :—

Bass. 3d. 2d. 1st. 5th.

(These notes represent the actual pitch of each of the five strings when tuned with piano or organ.)

There is no mystery about this; it is readily acquired and is not easily forgotten.

As playing the Banjo in combination with other instruments became popular, and as Banjo trios, quartettes and various combinations of Banjos became attractive features of concerts and musical entertainments, I became interested in seeking to produce a better combination of Banjos than were in vogue. The "Piccolo Banjo," a small instrument made to tune an octave above the ordinary Banjo, was well known. Its effectiveness is recognized in the " Banjo Club " and orchestra of Banjos.

In the fall of the year 1885, I devised, in order to produce certain effects, a Banjo having a large rim and a neck shorter in length than the diameter of its rim. This instrument I named the "Banjeaurine." Those who have perused the *Banjo Philosophically*, are familiar with the description of this instrument, which was most successfully introduced to the public by William A. Huntley and John H. Lee, those excellent performers, who used it, together with the ordinary Banjo (a Banjo of the dimensions of 11½-inch rim and 19-inch neck) in combination.

As I predicted two years ago, the form of my Banjeaurine has been duly imitated by several manufacturers of Banjos. They have also copied the name I gave to it— one firm only asking permission, the others appropriating it without. The metallic neck-adjuster, however, they have so far left alone, that being protected by letters patent in the United States.

The Banjeaurine is tuned *a fourth* higher than the Banjos which are tuned in "C and G." Thus the music intended to be played upon it in the " Banjo Orchestra " must be written a fourth lower or a fifth higher than the notation for the "ordinary Banjo." What is noted as the key of E for the " Banjeaurine " corresponds with the key noted as A for the " Banjo."

The question has been asked why I did not cause the Banjeaurine to be tuned a *fifth* instead of a *fourth* higher than the eleven or eleven and a half-inch rim Banjo, the length of string between the tail-piece and nut, by measurement, seemingly permitting such a pitch, even indicating it as proper.

I will, therefore, now explain to the reader why the Banjeaurine is tuned a fourth instead of a fifth above the Banjo.

First, I advocate stringing the Banjeaurine with a little heavier strings than the Banjo, for use in the "Banjo Club." The rate of vibration of a string is in inverse proportion to its thickness ; hence a slightly thicker string, on a short neck, is made to accord with a slightly thinner string on the same size neck. So that if the distance from the tail-piece to the nut on the Banjeaurine is about the same as the distance from the tail-piece to the 7th fret on the larger Banjo,* the difference between tuning a fourth and a fifth higher is allowed for by a slightly thicker string. In this tuning the *tension* of strings in the two instruments would be about the same.

Second, the Banjeaurine is, or was, originally intended for that class of music, in which the fourth string, called the bass string, is tuned a full tone higher than usual. Such music is generally marked "Bass to B," or "Elevate Bass." Now it is well known to Banjoists generally, that this pitch on the ordinary Banjo, when tuned in "C and G" is too high for the bass string, which is composed of silk, wrapped with wire. This pitch for the bass string being too high, and a great strain upon the string, causes it often to stretch so as to constantly lower in pitch until the strands of silk part. This being

*A string stopped at the 7th fret would sound a fifth above the open string.

the case, it were folly to establish a pitch for the Banjeaurine, which would leave it always open to this objection—the larger part of music being intended for it, necessitating this elevation of its bass string. So that, even when the Banjeaurine is strung with precisely the same strings as the ordinary Banjo, I concede the pitch I originally named for it the most applicable. ·

That excellent player, E. M. Hall, who rarely ever tunes the bass up to "B," played for some time on the stage, on a Banjeaurine of my manufacture, tuned a tone higher than I have advocated. But had he used the "elevated bass" he would not have been able to perform with pleasure, except in the clearest of weather. As it was, when summer came on, and murky weather appeared, he did, I believe, lower his tuning pitch * to that which I have advocated. Strings that will readily bear tuning high in a clear atmosphere, will not stand at the same pitch during murky or damp weather. It may be said that the Piccolo Banjo is open to objection on account of strings breaking; the pitch to which it is tuned—an octave higher than the C Banjo—being unnaturally high. This I will frankly admit. The Piccolo Banjo, as originally manufactured by myself, was made with a seven-inch rim, and a ten-inch neck, and was only intended for tuning an octave higher than the extra large B flat Banjo. Hence, I advocate a shorter string on the Piccolo Banjo, for to attempt a reconciliation by the use of a thinner string is almost folly—such thin strings, not resisting the necessary wear and tear of a musical performance in most cases. I have, in part, overcome the difficulty experienced in tuning, by shortening the necks one inch, and using a longer tail piece than formerly.

* Mr. Hall played the Banjeaurine with orchestral accompaniment.

## THE BASS BANJO,

recently gotten up to furnish deeper tones for the Banjo orchestra, consists of a large rim (sixteen inches in diameter), with an eighteen-inch neck, and is strung with very thick strings, such as are used on the Violincello; the third and fourth strings being of gut, wrapped with wire.* The Bass Banjo is conceded by Mr. Thomas J. Armstrong, the well-known teacher, and other prominent professors, to be a great assistance, and a valuable acquisition to the Banjo orchestra. Indeed, I had the honor of being the recipient of a vote of thanks, tendered by Mr. Armstrong's Banjo Orchestra of some sixteen members, only a few months ago, for an instrument of this description, manufactured for the use of said orchestra.

———

The Banjo as a solo instrument is a success. When accompanied by the guitar or piano, it is a decided success.

When used as an accompaniment to the voice in singing, it is always attractive. It has ever been conceded an excellent accompaniment.

When combined in numbers and sizes, Banjos may be used with striking effect, formed into an orchestra or band. It also has other uses—uses which many have not yet even dreamed of. One of them is as a medium for psycho-physiological curative agency. This may sound very strange to many readers, but instances of its usefulness in such direction are a matter of record.

———

* Strings are wrapped with wire to increase their density without, at the same time, adding much to their thickness. Prof. Tyndall says of such strings: " They resemble horses heavily jockeyed, and move more slowly (vibrate more slowly), on account of the greater weight imposed upon the force of tension."

A few years ago I preserved an account of a case where the Banjo was a medium of curative power. I will here append it. It was clipped from a medical journal.

"A case is reported of a lady, supposed to be dying of nervous exhaustion, being kept alive till she was fed and restored, by the persistent efforts of her attendant village doctor; who, lacking any other musical instrument, performed unceasingly for twenty-four hours by her bed-side on his Banjo, with appropriate gestures, till his patient awoke not only to life, but to a sense of the ludicrous, and revived in a fit of laughter.

Physiologists who never rest till they discover the reason why for all phenomena, have proved that music has undoubted influence on the circulation of men and animals, and that it accelerates the action of the heart; the variations in circulation being dependent on the pitch and loudness of the tone, and also on the timbre (character of tone). Music is thus placed in the list of physiological agents, and it may be made either useful or injurious, in certain diseased conditions, to humanity. Experiments are now being made on man and animals which will determine its value and influence more certainly in the future."

The writer of the foregoing evidently thought the Banjo only a second or third-rate instrument for use in such a case.; judging from the language in which the article is expressed, but we will pass that by.

Here again, it is found that science goes just so far and there stops. Medical science knows little, if anything at all, about the nervous circulation of men or animals, and I believe that the Hindoos, centuries ago, knew as much, or more, about the psycho-physiological action of music on men and animals as any modern physician knows to day. The powers and action of vibration are little understood by science to-day.

Music and the Banjo have their uses and they have their abuses. There is no power in existence, however good, which may not be perverted—and so inverted as to be abused.

There have been times within my own experience when music and the Banjo have been soothing and strengthening, refreshing me after a trying day's work. There have been other times when I could only listen to it with the greatest annoyance, and when it became wearisome and fatiguing. Musicians are, as a rule, sensitive—those who are not sensitive are not musicians.

Let the Banjoist study these conditions, and be governed by them. He may, with his Banjo, entertain, or he may annoy. Let him therefore, if he desires to cultivate his art, seek congenial musical associations and cultivate harmony within himself; for without harmony within there can be no true harmony without.

Let him avoid, if possible, coming in contact with those who seek only to display their imaginary skill, by pounding the strings with more muscular vigor than he possesses, and who seek in that way to "down him." Such persons have no true sense of harmony—their lives are made up of discord, and they must, through the perversity of their natures, manifest it in their Banjo-playing.

The "rough and tumble" class of Banjo-players is giving way to the rising school of artists. Therefore permit it to ebb away in peace—gentlemen should meet as gentlemen—musicians and artists, as musicians and artists. Thus only will the Banjo find its true sphere and retain it. Because it has been lowly—because it has come up from the depths—is no reason why it should not be honored and respected. The great oak was once but the little acorn—the greatest man who walks the earth was once only a little, weak, suckling child. Should he be despised because of this?

Let us, each and all, look to ourselves before casting sneers at that which is, or once was, lowly.

Let the Banjo continue to progress. Aid if you can, but hinder its progress—never

"*Non sum qualis eram.*"   I am not what I was,

## SECTION IV.

"The frets upon the viol were narrow ridges of wood, just raised above the finger-board, crossing it at right angles, and were so placed that the finger, casually falling between the frets, the string was stopped in tune. In the guitar they still remain as a guide to ignorance and an impediment to taste and expression." *Gardiner's Music of Nature.*

The foregoing lines are from *The Music of Nature* (a most valuable and highly-prized work), and have reference to the viol of the 16th century, of which the violin is an improvement.

The guitar, the mandolin and the zither are fretted instruments; they differ from the ancient viol inasmuch as the frets are of metal instead of wood. The violin, the 'cello, and the viola, are not fretted instruments, as is neither the double-bass. The guitarist or mandolinist who takes up the Banjo, most naturally desires frets, having been accustomed to them. The violinist, on the other hand, has been accustomed to the smooth finger-board, and therefore does not always take kindly to frets, perhaps considering them upon a Banjo, as Gardiner names them upon the guitar, "impediments," rather than aids.

Thus there has been a great difference of opinion as to which was best—the Banjo with smooth board, or the Banjo with raised frets. This difference of opinion has led often to hard feelings among Banjo-players; to many arguments, and has always been a cause of much annoyance to the manufacturer of Banjos. It is therefore hoped that the matter may be adjusted and reconciled.

I have at various times, and in various publications, made known my views, or the views held at that particular time, upon the subject of frets on the Banjo. I have now something further to say, and, indeed, the work would be incomplete were I to pass by, what I consider a subject of importance to the Banjoist, without some remarks upon fretted and unfretted finger-boards.

All violins are nearly of the same length from the nut to the bridge, and consequently of uniform length of vibrating string.* This being the case, the distance between the stops of the fingers are almost uniform on the different violins. Hence, a violinist by practice can accustom himself to fingering true, by the sense of touch or feeling, assisted by his ear. On the other hand, Banjos are made of various sizes, not only as regards length of neck, but also as regards the rim or body ; which causes a great difference in the position of the frets and fingering. As nearly all advanced players possess more than one Banjo—that is, use different sizes of Banjos for different kinds of musical effects,—to finger them accurately without some guide for the eye, becomes very difficult. Hence, all Banjos have what is termed "position marks" in the finger-board, and where frets are not laid across the surface of the board, they are generally, in one form or another, fixed at the side or edge of the neck. Were it not for this, a performer would be obliged to feel his way, and would often finger very inaccurately. With raised frets upon the finger-board, one has only to press the string between the frets and it is brought down upon the fret, so as to produce the desired note.

In the smooth finger-board playing, the string is pressed to the board with the finger, and, of course, must vibrate

---

* This, of course, has reference only to violins of full size. There are half-size and three-quarter violins made for boys.

between the bridge and the point at which it is stopped with the finger: the same when it is pressed upon the fret, but with this difference—the string in the one instance is stopped, as it were, with a soft pad (the end of the finger) and in the other instance is brought firmly upon a level metal surface; (the fret) which is claimed by many Banjo-players, to produce a *clearer* tone; and philosophically it should be so.

Now, applying Gardiner's theory to the Banjo,—that the frets on the guitar are a guide to ignorance and an impediment to taste and expression,—I assume that he would have included the Banjo with the guitar, provided there had been, in his day, any such instrument as our present Banjo. Assuming this, one naturally asks how correct such an opinion may be. Was the writer an authority? Was he a practical guitarist?

It is true that the smooth finger-board of the violin admits of wonderful effects, musical effects,—impossible with frets,—but these effects are possible only to the artist, and attainable only by constant study and incessant practice, assisted by a naturally correct musical ear.

The question is, is there sufficient musical power in the guitar to justify the immense amount of laborious practice necessary to enable one to finger it accurately without the aid of frets? It must also be remembered that to do so requires an unusual strength of the fingers of the left hand; for the fingering of chords and barrés upon the guitar is no easy matter, even with frets.

My own observation and experience leads me to assert that such an undertaking is extremely difficult and almost equal to waste of time. Now, on the Banjo, there is this difference: The strings used are thinner and more easily handled, and they are less in number, the four principal

---

* Raised frets are meant.

strings of the Banjo only being fingered with the left
hand. Therefore it becomes much easier to perform upon
a Banjo without frets* than upon a guitar without them ;
but it is, nevertheless, somewhat more difficult to learn
to play without the use of frets than it is with them.
The question then arises, is there any advantage in acquiring the power of playing on a Banjo without the
raised frets? I must reply that this is a matter of opinion ;
some really good performers asserting that the fretted
Banjo is preferable, and other equally good performers
asserting the contrary.  The frets, therefore, must have
their advantages and disadvantages, or there could not
be this difference of opinion among players.  These advantages and disadvantages I have at different times
commented upon in the columns of the *Banjo and
Guitar Journal.*  Suffice it to say here that with frets the
bridge of the Banjo must always remain in one particular
position upon the head of the Banjo ; any alteration in
its position altering the position of all the frets, for the
reason that the distance from the nut to the bridge, being
the full length of vibrating string, is divided upon known
principles of acoustics, to determine the position for each
fret.  Setting the bridge further forward, by shortening
the string, causes the frets to be placed nearer together ;
setting the bridge back, so as to lengthen the string,
necessitates the frets being further apart.  Hence, after
the position of the bridge has once been determined and
the instrument fretted, the position of the bridge cannot
be changed.

This fact alone is of no moment to many players, and
therefore will be counted as no objection ;  for only those
who sing songs and sometimes wish to quickly raise or
lower the pitch of their instrument by changing the
position of the bridge, care about moving or changing

the bridge's position on the head at all. Another objection to the frets is that they produce a "clanky" tone, devoid of expression. This I consider a grave objection in Banjos of large size, or those having long necks; but on the smaller Banjos, where the strings are shorter and more tense, a great deal of this "clank" is removed and the tone produced is very clear—especially nowadays, with our improved fretting wire, which is smoother and narrower than that used some years ago. In regard to the expression, or non-expression, that lies a great deal with the performer. There are some players who could not possibly perform with expression on a Banjo without frets; not possessing a sufficiently accurate musical ear. Such performers do better to use the fretted instrument. There are others, naturally endowed musically, and with ample time to devote to practice, who can as readily play on the smooth finger-board as with frets, and produce a great variety of musical effects, such as the "slide," etc.—to whom frets would be useless—purely an impediment to execution. But it is to be observed, that to produce a clear, full tone without the use of frets, necessitates firm fingers, which must be *hard* at the ends; which hardness, although it may be obtained by constant practice, is not always to be relied upon, for the hot weather of our summers tends to cause the fingers to soon soften, unless constant practice is kept up; and this practice, especially in the summer months, is not always followed.

Then again, all amateurs do not have the time to devote to this constant practice, and not only do the fingers soften, but inaccurate fingering also is a result.

Again, where one performs upon various Banjos of different sizes, accurate fingering upon each of them is very difficult without the use of frets—even so when

"dots," "smooth frets," or "position-marks" are used
as a guide to the eye; for the eye alone, or the ear alone,
cannot sufficiently control the arm, the hand and the
fingers to produce true stopping of the strings, unless
sufficient practice is indulged in to make those members
of the body act in harmony with the senses of sight and
hearing.

In my own experience I have found that playing upon
a guitar without frets was something too difficult to
accomplish, to warrant the necessary practice.   Playing
the Banjo without frets, I have found much easier; not
very difficult; not such a strain upon the fingers; not so
tiresome.   I have also found, that by practicing an hour
or so a day, I could handle almost any piece of Banjo
music as well on an unfretted Banjo, as upon a fretted
'Banjo; but when business made it impossible to keep up
my practice, I found that it was much more difficult to
play a new piece from the notes on an unfretted Banjo
than it was to play the same upon a Banjo having raised
frets.

Then again, in handling so many Banjos of different
sizes, changing from one size to another—a matter not to
be dispensed with in my business—I found made my
fingering upon an instrument with smooth board very
inaccurate, and accompanied by difficulties not experienced when playing constantly upon the one instrument.

These are the points, briefly given, which must be considered by the Banjoist; and he must, after considering,
decide for himself which is best.   But the beginner must
bear in mind, that after acquiring a knowledge of Banjo-
playing with the use of these mechanical helps, the
raised frets, it will be a matter of great difficulty for him
afterwards to learn to finger accurately without them,
should he at any time desire so to do.

This is an age of labor-saving machinery; and those who approve of the frets are becoming in the majority among the Banjo-players; but this of course does not decide the question as to which is best.

## FALSE STRINGS.

Strings which are not true in tone,—do not produce the proper notes when pressed upon the frets,—or which have an unclear and muffled tone,--are called "false strings." Such strings are one of the greatest impediments to playing upon fretted Banjos. (When the term "fretted Banjo" is used, *raised frets* are meant of course."

The laws—natural laws in acoustics—which govern the divisions of vibrating strings, making it possible to divide the length of string into sections, and decide the positions for the frets, are only applicable to vibrating strings when they are of *equal thickness* and of even density throughout their entire vibrating length. When a string—either upon the Banjo, the guitar, or any other instrument—is of uneven thickness, it will not vibrate perfectly, and will not produce true tones. Hence it is that many young students of the Banjo or guitar, upon getting a false string on their instrument, are led to suppose that the frets have, in some strange and peculiar manner, got out of place. Or, if it is a new instrument, they will some times send it to the manufacturer to have him ascertain what is wrong with it. Sometimes one is wise enough to change the string, which is most offensive, for another. Sometimes the other string proves to be even worse than the first, and then the uninitiated beginner is more perplexed than ever, and is ready to swear that the frets are wrong.

---

When a string is stoppéd—pressed to the finger-board, or upon the frets—midway between the nut and the

bridge; (which will be at the *twelfth fret*) the half of the
string should sound an octave higher than the open string;
the harmonic note produced at this fret, should also sound
an octave higher than the open string.* But it often
happens that the string is "false," and the position at
which it must be stopped, in order to produce the octave
note, sometimes varies, one way or the other, from one-
eighth to one-quarter of an inch, or more. With raised
frets this difference in fingering cannot be accomplished;
the nearest fret being the next possible stopping place.

Hence it is that many performers will not have raised
frets on a Banjo—because, if a string is false, but not too
false to be used—they can slightly change the position of
the fingering so as to make playing in tune upon such a
string possible.

Now some would say at once: Why not select only
strings which are true, and discard false strings? I must
reply that in the matter of Banjo-heads and Banjo-strings,
there are no infallible judges—one cannot always tell
what is true and what is false. If the unevenness in a
string is so great as to be seen or felt, the string should
be discarded; as there will be no use in taking the trouble
to put such a string on an instrument. But when the
unevenness is not perceptible, the string may yet be sufficiently false to cause trouble in playing. The only
redress a performer can have is to buy the best strings
he can get, and to select from them those which appear
to his judgement to be of even thickness, and free from
flaws.

There is one consolation which a performer of to-day
has over those of ten years ago; that is, that he can ob-

---

*See *An Exposition of the Harmonic Tones, and their
Philosophy*, by the author of this work. This treatise is bound
in with *The Banjo Philosophically*, and may be had for 10 cents.

tain strings at a much less cost. In fact, when I was an amateur, some years ago, I was obliged to pay just twice as much for Banjo-strings as Banjoists have to pay to-day, and the strings were no better, either.

## STRINGS TRUE AND STRINGS FALSE

Are manufactured in Germany. They are made from the intestines of young lambs. The manufacturers over there have a better climate for string-making than we have in America, and can also obtain suitable material; which cannot be obtained here, because lambs raised for the market are too fat and unsuitable for producing musical strings. It is an exceedingly difficult matter to manufacture, of gut, a string which is of perfectly even thickness throughout, and at the same time of sufficient strength and elasticity. Another thing, no two lots of material are alike, and it is therefore folly to suppose that any two lots of strings can be made alike. More-over, a change in the weather frequently occurs and spoils strings before they are entirely finished—the manufacture of them being carried on mostly in the open-air. The hot weather of our summers is very hard on strings, and attempts have been made to invent something superior to the material now used for making them, which would not be so readily affected by the weather; but so far without success. Silk strings are too soft; and through lack of hardness and elasticity, have not been a success. (This has no reference to the bass string, which is of silk, wound with wire.) Strings of steel wire have been tried and found useless on a Banjo—as have also strings made of brass wire. Wire strings are an abomination to a Banjo, and none but the worst of "plunkers" would care to use such. It is to be hoped that some enlightened American will yet invent a string which will have all the advantages, and fewer of the disadvantages, of the time-honored gut string.

It sometimes happens that the tail-piece of a Banjo will cut, or tear, a string near to the knot. When this occurs,—as is sometimes the case when the article is made of bone or ivory ;—a piece of "bass string" should be gently run through the holes in order to remove the sharp edge. A very soft string will frequently break at the tail-piece before it breaks elsewhere. A good ivory tail-piece, properly made, and having holes properly drilled, and all the sharp cutting edges removed, is as good a tail piece for all practical purposes as can be obtained.

Some years ago there was an improvement made in the fastening of piano strings, which are made of steel wire. In the old-fashioned way, a loop is made at the end of the string, which loops around a pin. In the new way, the loop goes around the pin and the string then makes a turn around another pin, the object being to divide the strain. This idea has of late been copied in tne form of Banjo tail-pieces ; but although their several inventors claim great improvement over the old style, I must confess that I have not found them any improvement whatever. Perhaps it is owing to the fact that I am careful to remove all the cutting edge from the holes in the tail-pieces I use. However that may be, I have certainly found that I could play about as long as anyone without having strings to break at the tail-piece, and, moreover, am able to adjust a new string about as quick, if not quicker, than can be done with the "patent tail-piece."

In *The Banjo Philosophically* I made some remarks concerning the care of the Banjo. These remarks have had, I am pleased to say, a good effect ; but it still remains a fact to my mind, that among the hundred thousand Banjo-players in this country to-day, there are not one hundred who understand how, or will take the trouble to keep their instrument in the best playing condition.

Unless the instrument is in proper condition, a good performance of the work intended for it cannot be expected.

Who would be fool enough to purchase a valuable race-horse and place him in the hands of an incompetent groom, or themselves neglect him, and then expect the animal to be in condition for the race-track?

And yet this is just about what many Banjo-players are doing to-day.

## THE BANJO IN CONDITION.

Some players who possess a variety of instruments will keep their violin and guitar in a suitable case, and their zither in a properly-lined box; their mandolin in a lined bag or leather case, and their Banjo hanging on the wall—(heavy side upwards, of course.)

The Banjo is not protected from the changes in the weather, and moreover, it frequently falls down from the wall to the floor, striking on the peg-head and splitting the neck.

There is no instrument in existence that is more easily affected by atmospheric changes than a Banjo. It is true that there is no delicate pine top to split, as there is in the guitar or mandolin; but there is the head, an animal substance, and a ready absorbent of moisture, which may be so impaired for the time being, that the Banjo is changed from a brilliant sounding instrument, to the veriest plunker.

Then there is the neck. Did you ever consider what a strain that delicate neck is daily subjected to? Not only is the constant tension of the strings to be considered; but also the plucking of those strings, as well as the pounding upon them (in some cases.)

Then there is the clumsy way in which some unskilled performers handle the pegs—shoving them into the holes by main strength ; and in doing this, pushing the neck upwards with a force which is calculated to strain any neck that can be made, out of position. It is no wonder then that the strain of the strings, together with the rough handling of some performers, causes the neck to spring forward, leaving a hollow in the fingerboard, which renders the instrument very difficult to perform upon. The thin necks made with some Banjos, to suit the delicate hands of certain performers, are not calculated to resist the inhuman handling of many of those who use them ; and no skill in manufacture—no seasoning of woods,—no amount of veneering of ebony, will prove an absolute preventive of warped necks if the instrument is not properly handled. You may just as well suppose that you can daily transgress nature's laws without in time having to pay the penalty, as to suppose that you can subject your musical instrument to improper handling and keep it for any length of time in playing condition.

The Banjo should be kept in a dry place, protected from any great dampness as well as from any great heat or cold. Cold is an absence of heat—heat is vibration. The head should be kept tight. As it stretches, use the wrench, a little at a time. It should be kept well strung, and the strings never loosened after playing—but kept in tune as nearly as possible. It does not hurt to allow the bridge to remain in position unless you are carrying the instrument about; in which case, I should advise the bridge being removed. A leather case, lined with flannel, is the best protector for a Banjo I can suggest; the best to carry the instrument in, and the best to keep it in at all times. The bolt which holds the tail-piece should never be screwed down tightly with the wrench, so as to cause the tail-piece to press, or lie upon the head. There should be sufficient space between it and the head to allow of a sheet of writing paper being passed under it, between it and the head. But, at the same time, if the tail-piece is so far up from the head that sufficient pressure is not brought to bear upon the bridge, the bridge will not stand in position upon the head in playing, nor will the tone be so good. Extremes in all things are to be avoided.

In regard to Banjo-necks, there never was a greater fallacy than to suppose that a neck made of walnut, rosewood, or other wood, and veneered with a thick strip of ebony, or other hard wood, will not warp. No one with any practical experience in making such necks, or in wood-working of similiar description, will attempt to maintain such an assertion. Walnut wood as well as rosewood, is porous, and of more or less open grain. Ebony is very hard and not at all porous. Walnut wood may be seasoned in the log, or in the plank, for many years, until it is "dry as a chip," and for all this, when it is sawed up into necks, or into pieces of suitable size for making necks, will begin to warp. Ebony, on the other hand, will not season, even if left to rest in the shape of logs for a generation or more. It must be sawed up into strips and allowed to dry out afterwards.

Now, when the hard ebony is glued upon the porous walnut, unless all the shrinkage has been got out of the wood, it is found that the necks will frequently warp, and the cause for this is found in the different shrinkage capacity of the two woods. Again, even when the woods have been, in both instances, seasoned for some time after being sawed out, unless the Banjo is taken proper care of and protected from dampness and changeable weather, there is a possibility of the neck warping. Few players are sufficiently familiar with these facts—or if familiar, pay sufficient heed to them—to keep their Banjos properly.

. Now.take, for instance, wood engravings. Everybody knows that the box-wood is so prepared by wedging, etc., for the making of such cuts, that any warping or changing in the wood is seemingly next to impossible. And yet, for all this, I have had fine wood cuts to warp on my hands. I have found that a certain number of such cuts, when enclosed for a length of time in a fire-proof vault, have warped; this, too, in a place which was supposed to be entirely free from all dampness. Any place, however, which is for any length of time closed so as to shut out all light of the sun, will generate a dampness, which is not only dangerous to the health of persons and animals, but likewise injurious to all else so secluded. Plants which are shut up from the light become tender and weak and must soon wilt and die. Therefore it is apparent that ventilation and sun-light are necessary to the health of the Banjo. I do not mean that the sun is to shed its rays directly upon the Banjo, and by reason of its too great heat, produce a contrary effect to that desired; but that a fair share of light and air is always desirable.

When the wood in the Banjo-neck has been properly seasoned and worked under the processes now recognized and found by years of experience to be proper, it will rarely warp when given proper attention and care; but no neck can be made to withstand the rough usage inflicted upon it by some of our players.

Banjo-heads, newly put on, will dry more rapidly and become sooner ready for use, when exposed to the air on a clear day. The sunlight will then absorb all moisture and carry it off. But heads will not properly dry on a wet day, or in very damp weather, even when placed near a stove. In fact, placing the rim with the new head upon it, near a stove, is never desirable at all—as the head will be caused to quickly contract, whilst the portion under the hoop and flesh-hoop remains wet or damp, and an unequal strain is thus brought to bear upon the head, which even if it does not break at once, will not last nearly so long as it otherwise would.

"All things were made for use, but none for abuse," and whilst a Banjo and a Banjo-head should bear all the wear and tear necessary to it as an instrument made for the use of man, it should not be abused.

### CONDITIONS NECESSARY TO A GOOD PERFORMANCE.

It has been my aim, for years, to bring the Banjo more into the parlor, and into the musical soiree; as I consider the conditions essential to a good performance more readily met with there, than in the theatre or concert hall.

It must be apparent to all observing minds, that the variety theatre, or even the minstrel hall, with their associations, are not the proper places for any musically inclined person to listen to an effective performance, musically, upon the Banjo. The majority of those who compose the audiences of such theatres, go there to be amused—to hear fun—and to laugh;—not to be entertained by music of a character such as those who attend more select musical entertainments, seek to hear and are desirous of listening to.

Hence it is that one rarely hears, on the minstrel or variety stage, a good rendition of instrumental Banjo music. There are some exceptions to this rule, but they are rare. Even when a really meritorious performer attempts to render musical effects of a more or less high order, on his Banjo, before a variety or minstrel audience, there are few who appreciate such a performance, and the " gods of the gallery " are frequently not slow in giving direct evidence of their dislike to anything pertaining to what some term a "classical performance." Hence, the Banjoist who is so unfortunate as to be compelled to gain a livlihood by following the minstrel or variety business, must—compelled by a necessity which recognizes no law—cater to the tastes of the majority ; however much it may be against the wishes of himself.

Therefore it is not surprising that frequenters of such places, having heard only comic songs, jigs, and perhaps a few marches, (" played in imitation of a brass band,") performed upon the Banjo, and frequently accompanied by the usual line of black-face " gags," etc., persist in declaring that the Banjo has no possibilities beyond those limited effects. Those who have heard the instrument under more favorable conditions are but a small number, compared with those who have never been permitted to enter within the " charmed circle," and listened to the instrument well played upon, accompanied by the piano.

It lies with the teacher,—who, by reason of being a teacher, must come in contact with many who desire to acquire a better knowledge of the capabilities and possibilities of the instrument,—to show to others (the friends and acquaintances of his pupils) that the Banjo has a higher sphere of usefulness and attractiveness. I have repeatedly pointed this out in my various writings, and am pleased here to record the fact that such work is being done in various parts of this country and in Europe.

Only a few days ago I received, direct from Paris, France, a letter from the young artist, Mr. De Witt C. Everest, in which he stated that at a private entertainment

in that city, there were some forty or more people of note
who came purposely to hear the American Banjo, and
that of this number, only one, a lady, had ever heard the
Banjo played before--or in fact—ever seen a Banjo.

" Countess ——," he writes, "said : 'What a lovely
instrument you have.  It sounds more like the harp than
any other instrument I have ever heard.'  Baron ——
said the same thing.  All were delighted."

Now does all this look as though the Banjo was fitted
only for the negro minstrels, or for the variety stage ?  No
thinking man or woman will continue to maintain such a
proposition after once becoming acquainted with the
facts ; and it is partly to make known such facts that I
have given this work to the public.

The parlor, the drawing room, and the select musical
entertainment being the proper places for the Banjo to be
rightly heard ;  it then remains to be observed that even
among the audiences of these entertainments will always
at times be found those who are not prepared to accept
the Banjo at once; as it deserves to be accepted, and
take immediately to music such as Themes, with variations, sets of Waltzes, Fantasias, etc., but who, at the
same time, will be immediately captivated, as it were, by
the rendition of some simple air played upon the Banjo,
with a like simple accompaniment on the piano.   Performances of " swinging solos," or " trick playing," with
the usual " juggling " of the instrument, seldom, if ever,
fail to at once convert those persons to an appreciation of
the merits of the Banjo.

Since the beginning of the world, history chronicles
the fact that people have ever been attracted by anything
like " wonders "—and by any and all things which appear to them to be out of the usual course of things.
Hence, a performance, in which the Banjo is sent twirl-

ing around the head,—or is swung in the air whilst playing some melody like the "Bell chimes imitation,"—often is astonishing to many who are not familiar with the extreme simplicity of the performance. I, myself, have often been called upon for a performance of this kind when playing in private, and have never yet found it otherwise than as I have stated.

After people have become a little more accustomed to hearing the Banjo played, they, not unfrequently, delight to listen to musical renditions of a somewhat higher order.

But there is such a thing as carrying the "classical" style of Banjo-playing too far, and of rushing into extremes. This is apparent when some otherwise competent players of the Banjo undertake to render a style or class of music which is not, properly speaking, Banjo music; music which is in any way adapted to the characteristics or capabilities of the instrument. Melodies like "Home, Sweet Home," for instance, with its variety of forms and styles of variations, is applicable to the Banjo—it is applicable to all instruments—and is effective; and so are many other musical compositions written for other instruments applicable to the Banjo. But there are some compositions, especially composed for the violin, the piano, or other instruments, which do not make the best selections to apply to the Banjo, and it is not always the question of *what can be done* on a Banjo, which can be hoped to entertain or attract an audience; but more frequently the question of bringing attractive music out of, or from the instrument, which is the desideratum to be accomplished.

Again, there is music—music especially composed for the Banjo—by competent players of that instrument, who, by reason of study and practice long in this one par-

ticular line of art, are competent to compose and construct that which is more effective, which can be played
with an effect upon the Banjo, that is likewise out of the
sphere and range of most other-instruments. Each
instrument must have its own independent sphere of
music, and each has some characteristic that another
has not. These points are to be considered by the
Banjoist who hopes to make his way with success in the
line of artistic Banjo-playing.

———

There are certain seasons of the year—such as our
American summers, for instance—when the Banjo is
often compelled to sound at its worst. No matter how
finished a performer may be, there are certain times when
surrounding or attending conditions make his perfor-
formance unsatisfactory to himself and to his audience.
When the air in summer is charged with a peculiar dampness, and the atmosphere is not only hot but humid, the
strings of the Banjo, like those of the violin, guitar and
harp, are caused to go out of tune easily, and what is
worse, to break very frequently. Not only does the air
itself act in a direct manner to cause this, but its action
upon the human body tends to moisten and make soft
the fingers, which, coming in constant contact with the
strings, has a bad influence upon them. This is discussed
more fully elsewhere.

It must also be remembered that no sound can travel
without a medium for its conduction, and that this
medium is the air, which is the vehicle of sound. The
reader has doubtless many times observed, that a Banjo
which sounds extremely loud and clear, when played upon
in a large, empty room; fails to sound either so loud or
so brilliant when the same room is filled with people.

This is even more apparent when the weather is damp,—
by reason of the dampness carried into the room by the
people.

Sound which moves uninterruptedly in a clear atmosphere has much advantage over the same sound when i
is compelled to move in a dense atmosphere, or is im-
peded in its course by a mass of living bodies, or even of
thick carpets, curtains, furnitnre, etc. This is a subject
which belongs to acoustics, and as there are so many
excellent works written upon it, and similar subjects; in
which the reader can easily gain all the information desired, I will not go deeper into it here.

The humidity in the air in summer,—upon certain
days,—renders a favorable performance upon the Banjo
very uncertain, not to say impossible. But the winter
seasons have altogether the opposite effect, furnishing a
clear, cold atmosphere, not only favorable to the trans-
mission of sound, but in every way favorable to this particular instrument, the Banjo. The head, in cool weather,
remains more firm and hard, and the strings are not so
liable to break, and are more likely to stand in tune.
Not only is this the case, but the fingers of the performer,
remaining free from perspiration, have not the tendency
to break or soften the strings which they have in the hot,
humid months. It is then, during the seasons of fall,
winter, and spring, that the Banjoist finds the greatest
satisfaction in his Banjo performances. These are the
seasons favorable to Banjo performances of all kinds.

### COMIC BANJO-PLAYING.

I do not wish it to be thought that I disparage Banjo-
playing in a "black face," nor do I wish to cast any slurs
at the performer who makes use of his Banjo for a
"comic act,"—as an accompaniment to comic songs, etc.

Comic songs are often amusing, and a really comic Banjo act is often highly entertaining. But all things must change. A Banjo performer who years ago could —upon the minstrel stage,—entertain an audience and command a good salary, by singing negro songs; would not meet with much success to-day; nor could he command any salary to speak of. The people of to-day have wearied of the monotonous songs of the darkey; and when they listen to comic songs, they want, at the same time, to listen to "hits at the times," political and otherwise. The ludicrous must be intermingled with other effects than musical, if the mass of frequenters of variety or minstrel halls are to be entertained. One cannot live always without fun in this world: there is an old saying, "Laugh and grow fat," which may not be altogether bad advice for some of us to take, although we may not all desire to be corpulent. However,

"A little nonsense now and then,
Is relished by the best of men."

Comic songs are very good in their place, and there are very many persons who delight to listen to a really good comic song, accompanied by the Banjo. But what would you have thought to have seen Ole Bull, Vieuxtemps, or any of our modern violin virtuosi, appear on the stage in black face and attempt to render their almost supernal music in that disguise?

The mask of cork, you would doubtless say, was not the proper thing to wear on such an occasion; nor in any way in affinity with the music produced.

Hence, I think that the higher grade of Banjo music is better performed in evening dress, or in plain citizens' clothes, with the face and hands in their natural color and condition; and that this class of Banjo music should be separated from the comic sort.

This may be only an opinion of my own, but I believe
there are many excellent Banjo-players who entertain
somewhat similar views

## "NUDIS VERBIS."

## SECTION V.

" Well, sir! Now I've heard what you had to say:—I would like to know what others have to say about it—I mean the Banjo." Section V, then, will tell you a little of what others have said.

Now that I have given some of my own personal views concerning the Banjo, it may not be out of place to append the views and opinions of the *literati* of the day— the same clipped from various newspapers, published in different places and under various dates. I feel that my work without this would be very incomplete.

Extracts from the press, together with some comments upon them, I therefore utilize in this section of the work; trusting they may be of interest to such as are not familiar with the Banjo and its present stage of advancement in the sphere of music and art. Opinions are, of course, but *opinions*, and from whomsoever they may come must be considered as opinions only.

An article concerning the Banjo, from the St. Louis *Critic* of Sept. 5, 1886, reads as follows:

" Ten years ago the idea of discussing the Banjo in a serious article on music would have been laughed at by ninety-nine out of a hundred of our musical people. To-day it would be a serious oversight if one should take no account of this popular musical instrument. Dame Fashion has made it popular, and now its merry 'twang' is heard in many a parlor, from which but a short time ago it would have been flung out in disgrace. Like the fiddle, the Banjo got into disrepute because it was played by people whom the aristocracy do not usually associate with. Perhaps it will never cease to be frowned upon by the

puritanical till, like the fiddle, it gets a new and more aristocratic
name. One curious feature of the growth in popularity of the
Banjo is the way the ladies have falllen in love with it. Indeed
it has so many devotees among the fair sex that Banjo clubs have
been formed in many cities. Boston, New York, Philadelphia
and Chicago have clubs composed of ladies of the highest social
position. In London, Lady Fanny Cowper, a grand-niece of
Lord Palmerston, gave a very fashionable concert, in which she
was assisted by eleven young ladies, all playing on the Banjo.
When Christine Nillson came to this country, one of her first
achievements was to learn how to play the Banjo. She 'picked'
the Banjo with gusto in her leisure moments, and one of the
prettiest sights was to see the great prima donna romping with
little children and playing the Banjo for them with the skill of
an expert. Clara Louise Kellogg is another of the prima donne
who has a fondness for the Banjo, and during Miss Ellen
Terry's visit to this country she became fascinated with its
melody, and took lessons of a leading teacher until she became
an adept in its use, and the tinkling of the Banjo is often heard
in her apartment. E. L. Davenport was an enthusiastic Banjo-
player, and his daughter Fanny is also an expert. Mary Ander-
son has caught the fever and Lawrence Barrett's daughter is a
fine performer. No doubt it was Lotta's Banjo-playing that
started the popularity of the instrument among 'professionals'
and those connected with them. Now, however, there are many
ladies playing the Banjo who know the stage only from the front
side of the foot-lights, and there seems to be no reason why they
should not, for the Banjo has many qualities that make it a delightful feature of the home. In the Eastern cities a gentle-
woman's boudoir or music-room is not complete without a Banjo,
and its study forms a part of the curriculum of almost every
school-girl, and at the summer resorts you will hear its 'jingle'
wafted out upon the air from the windows of the hotels and
cottages. The fair sex, however, do not have an entire mon-
opoly of the instrument, for stronger hands than theirs often

'pick' the strings, and society young gentlemen are most desirable when they can accompany their lady friends on the Banjo. The money expended in the purchase of Banjos would hardly be credited were the amount to be set down in cold figures."

I have already alluded to the success made by an American Banjo-player in London, England, in the year 1880, the celebrated Banjoist, E. M. Hall, who left America to fill an engagement with the Moore and Burgess Minstrels, at St. James' Hall.

Concerning his appearance there, the London *Era* had the following, by which it will appear that no artist in music since the time of the famous Paganini, has achieved a more striking success. In fact, the Banjo-playing of E. M. Hall was a revelation to the Britishers, and there can be but one possible plea of objection by the "holier than thou" class of musicians, which is, that his act was done in "black face," and among minstrels, instead of upon the legitimate concert stage.

"Mr. E. M. Hall has made an extraordinary hit with his Banjo-playing. He may be called the Paganini of the Banjo, for never before have we heard that instrument manipulated in such an artistic style. There is a kind of fantastic poetry in the way Mr. Hall plays the Banjo. He makes the instrument produce both pathetic and humorous effects of the most novel kind. In his principal solo, a sort of caricature of Thalberg's variations on the popular melody 'Home, Sweet Home,' Mr. Hall introduced some of the most original passages we have ever heard upon the Banjo or any other instrument. Keeping the melody all the time, he played an accompaniment on the other strings, and showing variations full of difficulties. Scales, chromatic passages, startling intervals extending over several octaves, chords, shakes—in fact, every kind of musical effect to be obtained by a skillful pianist or violinist can be produced by Mr. Hall; and one of the most remarkable features of the solo was a variation, in which the air was played with a tremolo effect, whilst it was accompanied with chords. Mr. Hall has evidently decided genius for music, and we fancy he could easily become a master of almost any other instrument; but seeing what amusing, extraordinary and original playing he introduces on the Banjo, one could hardly wish him to change. The rule against encores was obliged to be set aside, so delighted were the visitors with his solo."

The following is another item clipped from the St. Louis *Critic :*

" E. M. Hall, the wonderful Banjoist, gave a private reception at the St. James Hotel last week, complimentary to Miss Ada McClelland of this city. Mr. Hall played 'Home, Sweet Home,' with variations, an arrangement that gave him his name, the 'King of the Banjo.' The theme was played in a low, sweet strain, and the variations with such exquisite precision and rapidity as to excite the wonder of his listeners. To Mr. Hall the Banjo, to a great extent, owes its growing popularity as a solo instrument. Not only has his wonderful performances been received with favor throughout this country and Europe, but his compositions are popular and in the library of every professional and amateur. They are easy of execution, brilliant in effect and perfect in harmony.

Miss McClelland has her class nearly full for the fall term, which begins in September. Many of our society ladies will begin practice on the Banjo, which appears to be the favorite instrument."

The *Critic*, as may be seen, speaks in the same language of Mr. Hall's playing of his famous *Home, Sweet Home*, as did the London *Era*, previously alluded to. There are many expert performers on other instruments who would be only too proud of similar press notices if they could but get them.

Another issue of the same paper says :

" During the past three years the Banjo has become the favorite instrument among the young people of both sexes all over the country. Particularly is this true in the large cities and among the wealthy classes. No longer is it connected in the mind with negro minstrels and Southern plantation scenes, but holds rank equal with the violin and the guitar."

Those who still assert that the Banjo possesses no musical merit, will be compelled now to face those of another opinion—and "those of another opinion " will prove to be largely in the majority.

The following is from the *N. Y. Morning Journal*, under date of November 27, 1887 :—

" The Banjo has undergone many changes since its ' plunks ' used to ring out on the moonlit air along Mississippi levees on summer nights befo' de wah. The earliest recollections of the instrument, which have been handed down to us show it to have been originally made of a cheese box or a peck measure for a rim, while the head was of sheepskin, cemented or tacked to the rim, but much coarser than that which is at present in vogue, and the handle was of rough-hewn hickory. The strings were of catgut, and resembled small-sized ropes. Altogether it looked more like a heavy wedge mallet than a musical instrument.

The origin of the Banjo is somewhat doubtful. Those who know about all there is to know of it to-day are little informed as to its early history. By some it is said to have originated in Spain, being an evolution of the mandolin. Those in favor of this theory point to a Spanish painting of the sixteenth century, in which one of the figures holds a Banjo in his hand. But this theory is pooh-poohed by those who claim that the Banjo found its birthplace in Africa and was transplanted in this country by the natives who were brought here in slavery.

Whatever the truth may be in regard to its origin it has certainly always been an instrument in high favor with the negro, and, in fact, an instrument for the playing of which the colored race has always shown a natural aptitude. Could some of the dusky plunkers of the old days see the handsome, symmetrical instrument called the modern Banjo, they would not believe it to be the same which once gave so much joy to their leisure hours.

The ordinary Banjo of to-day consists of a rim generally made of German silver, with wooden band inside. A steel or brass wire rests upon the same, and the head, which is either of sheep or calf-skin, is held in place by a band connected with brackets attached to the rim. The handle or neck, as it may be called, is made of rosewood or mahogany, while snakewood is sometimes employed. Most handles are fretted, but advanced players use the Banjo without frets, as practice brings an instinctive knowledge of the exact point at which to finger in order to produce a given tone.

It is only within the last few years that the Banjo has become a drawing-room instrument. In this respect it has gradually supplanted the guitar. Many prominent society ladies are numbered among the devotees of the Banjo. Ladies are said to be more apt pupils. The light touch, which is the modern method, and which produces the acute tones necessary to good playing, appears to be especially easy of accomplishment by the ladies. Besides this, teachers say they pay better attention to instructions and put heart into their work.

The Banjo is becoming such a general accomplishment that the young lady puts forth extra effort to master it. In a few years the young lady who can't plunk the Banjo will be as uninteresting as the one who formerly could not play the piano.

The Banjo is especially adapted to accompany the voice in song. It matters little what may be the character of the composition. It lends life and spirit to the rollicking ditty of the ministrel and adds pathos to the musical romance.

For purely instrumental effects its scope is unlimited. In the hands of a skilled player the most difficult compositions can be faithfully rendered. The rage now among lady and gentlemen Banjoists is 'The Marriage Bells,' 'The Dead March,' from 'Marionette,' and selections from the light operas. 'Home, Sweet Home' admits of many variations, and some players can permeate the air with more wonderful intricacies than are possible on any other instrument.

The methods of the old minstrel performers, who wore a thimble on the index finger, and thumped with more or less vigor, has given way to the more delicate 'pick' with the bare fingers among modern players. Of course the old-timers disparage this 'dude' touch, as they term it, and say, with Horace Weston, the most prominent exponent of the 'tump,' that it is all wrong. But young ladies, who, with their delicate touch charm drawing-room auditors, know how much more efficacious is the modern 'pick' in charming their music-loving hearers."

The assertion of the writer of the foregoing, that the Banjo is especially adapted to accompany the voice in songs of whatever character, is well attested. But when he says that "for purely instrumental effects its scope is *unlimited*," he makes even a stronger plea for the Banjo than I myself do. However, it is well.

Bnt I must differ with the writer regarding the playing of that famous colored artist, Horace Weston. Anyone who asserts that Weston declares against the guitar style, or "picking" of the Banjo, shows himself to be unfamiliar with the playing of that artist. I have heard Weston pick the Banjo in a manner that would astonish many. I have heard him pick with so delicate, and at the same time, so brilliant a touch that one would scarcely believe the instrument he was manipulating could possibly be a Banjo. Likewise I have heard him "strike," or thimble, in the same delicate and artistic manner, where most other players could produce only a hard thumping noise. I do not doubt that he can "thump," and thump hard, when occasion requires,—and the occasion requiring such thumping is generally the bar-room and its associates,—where perhaps our worthy writer may have had the misfortune to hear him play. I who am familiar with the playing of Horace Weston in all its branches, must bear record to the fact that I have heard no one who can excel him in artistic execution when *he is permitted to perform under proper conditions.*

I must also take exception to the remarks of the *Morning Journal* correspondent, that "advanced players use the Banjo without frets, as *practice brings an instinctive knowledge of the exact point at which to finger in order to produce a given tone.*"

Practice produces no *instinct*, for instinct is something inborn in men and animals. In fact, not one player in a hundred ever plays without "frets" of some kind, even though concealed from the eye of the auditor.

---

Concerning a soiree musicale, given by Miss Everest, of Philadelphia, in March, 1888, where the Banjo Quartette of Mr. D. C. Everest took part, a musical journal had the following:

"While the style of music evolved from the Banjo was hardly up to the standard of the balance of the programme, it was evident that the rendition did not fail in amusing the audience."

What would the worthy reporter of that particular journal have to say about a cornet soloist's performances at such a concert? He would doubtless consider such tunes as Yankee Doodle, with variations, classical, provided they came from a horn instead of from the Banjo. At any rate, he states that the Banjo music *amused the audience*, which is doubtless more than he himself could have accomplished with any instrument.

Not far from here, about this time, there were other Banjo performances taking place. One of these was a grand concert, given in Boston, Mass., in Tremont Temple, on the evening of December 14, 1887.

Let me read you what the well-known paper, the Boston *Herald*, had to say concerning it: There were sixty Banjos on the stage in the Banjo Orchestra:—

"It was a festival night for Banjoists at Tremont Temple last evening, and the twing twing, twang twang, thumb thumb of the popular instrument of the day was heard by the immense audience present for two hours, varied only by occasional interruptions by a glee club and a humorist. The procession of Banjo-players that filed into the building singly, in couples and in crowds astonished and puzzled the ordinary passers through Tremont street, and created a great excitement among the favored ticket holders. The idea of massing all the available Banjo talent of the town and giving a concert with a Banjo 'orchestra' originated with the members of the Boston Ideal Banjo, Mandolin and Guitar Club, and the result attending the carrying out of their idea was certainly interesting to those who attended last evening. Mr. William A. Huntley was the star artist of the evening, and the solo talent, in the line of Banjo-playing, included Miss Vena Robinson, Miss Flossie Southward and Miss Marie Thresher. The Longwood club and the Freshmen Club from Harvard College also took part in the programme as well as a miscellaneous 'orchestra' of over three score players, the Lotus Glee Club and Mr. Edward T. Phelan, humorist, assisting. The great 'act' of the evening was the appearance of the 'orchestra,' which, under Mr. George L. Lansing's direction, played Shattuck's 'Invincible Guard March,' with splendid precision, creating the most novel and enjoyable effect. The Ideal Club, which has been heard frequently in and about the city this season, made another brilliant success, and both the Longwood and the Freshmen Clubs played with highly commendable skill. Mr. William A. Huntley again showed himself an accomplished soloist, and was enthusiastically applauded for each and all of his selections.  Miss Thresher, six years old, gave evidence of early talent, and the other soloists, also of tender years, acquitted themselves with credit.  Mr. Phelan is a very clever imitator, and his contributions to the entertainment were greatly enjoyed, as were also the members introduced by the glee club.  Altogether, the concert made quite a new departure in Banjo-playing, and proved that the instrument can be used with advantage in many combinations suited to the concert-hall."

It will be observed that this well-known and ably conducted paper, says, that the concert "*proved that the instrument can be used with advantage in many combinations suited to the concert-hall.*"

In the face of such testimony none but a blind musical bigot will continue to assert that the Banjo *has no music in it.*

"The American Banjo Club," led by Mr. T. J. Armstrong, gave a concert in Philadelphia on the evening of December 19, 1887.  It was largely attended, being the first entertainment of the kind given in Philadelphia. There were sixteen Banjos in the Banjo Orchestra.  Miss Edith E. Secor, an accomplished lady Banjoist, played solos, accompanied by her sister on the piano.

The Philadelphia *News* published the following notice concerning this concert :

"The Banjo concert at Association Hall last evening was a decided success.  It was given to a large audience, who knew for the first the amount of music that could be knocked out of the plantation instrument."

The *Item* has the following :

"The performance of the Banjo Club, which appeared three times during the evening, was in every way admirable, showing careful and effective training, and a thorough mastery of the instruments used."

The *Sunday Times* had the following :

"A REVELATION IN BANJO MUSIC."

"On last Monday evening at Association Hall a grand novelty concert was given by the American Banjo Club under the able direction of Thomas J. Armstrong. The concert, it is said, was the first of its kind ever given in this city, and was certainly a revelation in Banjo music."

Concerning the playing of that wonderful man, Horace Weston, we have seen much in the papers, but none of the accounts go a step beyond what I have really heard him do. In fact, he is even a better player than any of the papers have ever stated. The only newspaper notice of him, or his playing, that I have by me at present, is the following, which I clipped from the *Yale News*, of December 8, 1881, a paper which is, I believe, published by the Yale College students :

"There is so much interest taken in Banjo-playing in college that those who are really fond of fine playing would like to have a chance to hear the world-renowned 'banjoist,' Horace Weston who is now taking a rest in New Haven, after a two years' trip around the world. We have heard several Banjo-players who were considered fine, but not one of them could compare with Weston. We would like very much to hear him again, and if the manager of the American Theatre were to engage him, he would be sure of a crowd of students to hear this really magnificent musician. Weston, though colored, can play the Banjo in a way no other man of any complexion whatsoever ever pretended to. We hope there will be an opportunity to hear some of his playing."

----

The following brief notices taken from the papers to which they are credited, attest to the merits of the Banjo and guitar in the hands of John E. Henning and his accomplished wife :

"The seven hundred guests at the Long Beach Hotel, L. I., were delightfully entertained Monday evening by the J. E. Henning Banjo and Guitar Concert Co. It proved to be the great event of the season."—*N. Y. Tribune.*

"John and Meta Henning gave one of their delightful Banjo and guitar entertainments at Walton Place, Thursday evening, for the benefit of the Choir Fund of the Church of the Ascension. It was a great success, as it always is when those wonderful people are advertised."—*Chicago Tribune.*

Thousands of similar press notices could be given.

———

In Providence, R. I., on the evening of May 16, 1888, a concert was given before an audience of 2000 people. Fifty Banjo-players appeared on the stage in the Banjo Orchestra.

The *Evening Telegram* had the following:

"Mr. Huntley, of course, was the leading figure of the evening. He is a marvellous Banjo-player and seems to possess a certain power over the instrument that no other artist has ever shown here. He plays with good taste, his ideas are original, and he makes the instrument fairly speak. The encores were extremely hearty and he responded with some very choice selections. The Boston Club played magnificently and were received with enthusiasm."

The Banjo is all right. What we want is only a few more such players as Mr. Huntley, who is an artist in every sense of the word.

The Providence *Journal* of April 16, 1888, in speaking of a concert given by Reeves' Band at Low's Opera House, says: "The Banjo and guitar playing of the Boston Ideal Club was one of the gems of the concert." As Reeves' Band is one of the finest in this country, this is saying a good deal for the Banjo.

An English musician has the following to say concerning Banjo-playing:

LUSBY'S WINTER PALACE.

LONDON, ENG., Nov. 9, 1882.

" In the course of my professional duties I have often listened to performances on the Banjo, although I must confess on these occasions my sentiments were not always pleasurable, but after having heard Mr. Turner play, both in public and private, I must honestly say that in his hands the Banjo completely changes its nature; from an instrument of thin tone and limited capabilities it becomes a powerful solo instrument and rich in harmony.

His manipulation is marvelous and his memory inexhaustible; in fact, it is well worth the while of any musician to see Mr. Turner and hear how an artist can overcome the difficulties even of this instrument.

CHARLES BELL, Musical Director,
Royal Academy of Musicians."

All this goes to demonstrate that those who assert that the Banjo is not a musical instrument have spoken ignorantly. When two or three persons can testify under the law to having been witnesses of a certain transaction, their testimony goes further than that of thousands of others who can testify that they knew nothing of said transaction, not having been present.

The testimony of a few reliable and qualified witnesses that there is music,—and good music,—in the Banjo, is worth all the contrary opinions of those who have never heard the instrument properly played upon, and therefore assert to the contrary.

Although I am not, myself, "in the field" as a Banjo-player,—having my hands full of other matters and little time for practice,—yet I have had the pleasure on hundreds of occasions, of astonishing those who had never

before heard the Banjo properly played ; or never heard
it played at all with an accompaniment on the piano.
I have never yet found a single person who was at all
musically inclined that did not " fall in love" with the
music produced by the Banjo and piano. Thus I can
say truly that *it needs only to be heard.* There are
thousands upon thousands who have never heard the
Banjo properly played, or ever examined a good instrument in the shape of a Banjo.

"The Banjo is an older instrument than the violin. Long
before the violin was thought of, the heathen on the banks of the
Congo, civilized people on the banks of the Nile, and others more
or less civilized, from China to the Atlantic, played the Banjo.
The Egyptians were great Banjo players, and so were the people
of Africa, and it was natural then that the African when brought
to this country should introduce to us their time-honored instrument."—St. Louis *Critic.*

The following brief notice,—brief, but to the point,—is
taken from a paper published in Arkansas, the *Judsonia
Advance,* and relates to a telegraph operator in that
locality, who has been playing the Banjo for some time.

"Our new night operator at this place, Mr. S. B. Fraser, is an
accomplished Banjo-player. Many people think that the Banjo
is an instrument for the negro or minstrel entertainment, but
after listening to his rendition of difficult instrumental music on
the Banjo they will change their minds very materially."

This is similar to the evidence I am constantly coming
in contact with,—from the press and from musicians,—
that the Banjo needs only to be properly heard in order
to be appreciated. I am glad to be able to record the
name of Mr. Fraser in this little work, and will be pleased
to know, at all times, that others are handling the instrument with the same skill.

Mr. Wm. A. Huntley once remarked to me that he
thought so much of a Banjo, that he wanted one carved
upon his tomb-stone when he died. This is the secret of
his (Mr. Huntley's) power over the instrument: Love—
inherent love for his favorite instrument—inspiring him
to practice and work.

Quite different is it with those who care only for the
instrument as a means of making a livelihood, or getting
money; they are never true artists in music, having no
real love for it.

Said a "simple method" teacher to me once: "The
Banjo has come up quick, and it will go down quick."
There was not enough money in it to keep him longer in
the business of teaching and selling inferior Banjos. He
had never worked for its upward course; caring only to
get money from ignorant persons in exchange for cheaply-
made Banjos, and still worse music. He was therefore
little qualified to predict or judge as to what the future
had in store for the Banjo. The less number of such
persons we have in the business, the better for all concerned.

----

"While some hypercritical persons are fond of pelting with
saitre and obloquy those of their countrymen and women who
carry their admiration of English customs and manners to the
extremes of plagiarism, it is some slight satisfaction to know that
more than one American institution has found its way across the
Atlantic, and has made a home for itself among the inhabitants
of 'perfide Albion.' The very latest craze among the British
aristocracy is the Banjo. The colored brothers Bohee are at
home in many of the most high-class boudoirs and drawing-
rooms in London. STEWART, OF PHILADELPHIA,
Dobson of this city, besides many native professors, of whom
perhaps Harry Spratt is the most popular, are all in large way of

business, teaching dukes and duchesses, lords and ladies, the mysteries of 'picking' and the use of the thimble. The craze received quite a fillip a short while since by an order to Harry Spratt direct from his Royal Highness Prince Albert Victor of Wales for a Banjo, and to wait upon him to give him lessons upon the instrument. The English are rapidly becoming Americanized."—*The Press*, New York, March 6th.

The foregoing may be of interest : Whilst we Americans imitate the English with our bob-tail saddle horses, etc., they are not slow to imitate us in many things. There are a number of teachers of the Banjo in London and other cities and towns in England, and many of them are liberally patronized. I, myself, have supplied hundreds of instruments to English ladies and gentlemen and am safe in asserting that the " English Banjo," with its six and seven strings, is rapidly being superseded by our American five-string Banjo. However, readers of my *Banjo and Guitar Journal* are well acquainted with all such facts.

The following is from *The Indicator*, Chicago, under date of August 11th, 1888. The *Indicator* is one of the best musical journals in America :

" We have received from S. S. Stewart, of Philadelphia, copies of his *Banjo and Guitar Journal* for several months of the present year; also a copy of a lecture by himself upon " The Banjo Philosophically; " also a price list of Stewart's Parlor, Concert and Orchestra Banjos, and a very full and complete list of musical publications—sheet music, instruction books, etc.—for students of the Banjo. The *Journal* contains a vast amount of information suitable to all who take an interest in this famous instrument, together with many choice musical exercises."

It will be seen that the Banjo, as an instrument, is not tabooed by the musical press as it was some years ago.

The following is from the L. I. *Times*, of Dec. 27, 1883. The gentleman referred to is well known as a writer of Banjo music :

" Musicians all over the country have been greatly interested in Mr. A. Baur's attempts to secure for the somewhat plebeian Banjo a place among the great musical instruments. Mr. Baur has contended that the power and scope of the Banjo has never been appreciated, and that it is capable of interpreting the finest music with as much effect not only upon the ear, but upon the heart and mind as any instrument invented. He has backed his theories by proofs which have won the regard and consideration of eminent artists and critics. He has arranged the most pretentious music for the Banjo, and has executed the most difficult chords and the most passionate strains with startling effect. It is being very generally conceded that his experiments are wonderfully successful. Certainly he has created a revolution in the kind of music now being played upon the Banjo, and has, at the same time, won for his commanding genius an esteem which will soon cause his name to be long remembered as an artist of rare and original ability."

The following is an extract from the *Journal*, Flushing, L. I., under date of Dec. 22, 1883 :

" When Mr. Baur, the Banjoist, appeared on the stage, he was greeted with vociferous applause, and as he moved his dexterous fingers over the strings, almost a death-like stillness pervaded the house. The music was exquisite, and Mr. Baur was encored three times."

How different all this reads from the attacks of over-zealous persons who assert that the Banjo possesses no musical merit whatever, and is fit only for the accompaniment of simple songs.

" The heretofore despised Banjo is to be elevated to the first rank as a musical instrument. Some one has discovered that it is of very ancient origin, and, of course, that is very much in its favor, as many persons delight in anything that is associated with antiquity. A relic-hunter in Egypt found, or says he found, in the tomb of a royal family, in one of the oldest pyramids, a Banjo of the exact form of those played by plantation darkies. In his opinion the ancient Pharoahs delighted in the sweet sounds produced by the Banjo, which constituted the favorite music of the country which has been called the cradle of civilization."— From the Philadelphia *Evening Star*, Oct. 27, 1881.

That there is a great deal of truth in the foregoing item I do not deny. People nowadays love to copy after the antique, and as I myself have stated, in the language of another, "History repeats itself." and the Banjo will most surely find its way to the front. It appears to be the will of the gods of music, and of art, that this is to be accomplished.

And yet there are some persons who really do not know the difference between a Banjo and a tambourine.

"There is good reason for believing that the heretofore despised Banjo is to be elevated to the first rank as a musical instrument. Some one has discovered that it is of very ancient origin, and of course that is much in its favor, as many persons delight in anything associated with antiquity. A relic-hunter in Egypt found, or says that he found, in the tomb of a royal family, in one of the oldest pyramids, a Banjo of the exact form of those played by the plantation darkies. In his opinion the ancient Pharoahs delighted in the sweet sounds produced by the Banjo, which constituted the favorite music of the country which has been called the cradle of civilization. It is easy to account for the introduction of the Banjo into this country. It was brought by the negroes from Egypt by way of Ethiopia. Many people will now admire the Banjo who despised it when it was thought to be the invention of some negro barbarian. Indeed, it is stated, very aristocratic people, as well as many accomplished musicians, have long been pleased with the Banjo, and that the latter have played it 'on the sly.' Lord Dunraven, of England, is said to be an accomplished Banjo-player. Thalberg, the pianist, Miss Nillsson and Clara Louise Kellogg, the opera singers, are also enthusiastic lovers of the ancient Egyptian instruments. A London musical instrument maker states that he cannot supply the demand for the fashionable rival to the piano."—*Washington Capitol.*

The foregoing is very good, although much like what has previously been said.

" A Banjo-player in Cincinnati killed a girl by striking her on the head with his Banjo. So even the Banjo has its uses. We have heard murders committed with it before."

The above is from *The Score*, August, 1880. We have heard murders committed with it also, and they would have greatly increased had such papers as the *Score* had control of the instrument.

The following, however, is somewhat of a different nature, being another account of the restoration to health of a sick person.

It is from a paper called the *Merrimac Valley Visitor*, published in Newburyport, Mass., under date of December 11, 1880.

" A queer case of awakening the mental powers occurred a time since in the Ipswich asylum for the insane. A boy was there who gave only the least possible indications of being above the brute creation, if indeed he was up to the highest standard of irrational animal life. He had no conversational powers, could not answer the simplest question, and took little or no notice of passing events. One day a Banjo-player came along, and Dr. Hurd, as his custom is, employed him to play a time for the amusement of his patients. To the sound of the first notes this idiotic lad gave attention; and shortly ran to the player's side and looked intently at every motion he made. He was perfectly fascinated; and there sprang into wakefulness powers till then dormant, which grew beneath the doctor's care till he was restored to reason, discharged from the asylum, and able to support himself. The mere animal was aroused to human life; and a soul hidden under the grossest covering was revealed and started on the journey of eternal life."

Here we have the case of a child who was not merely physically diseased, but also mentally undeveloped. Probably, had it not been for the Banjo, he would have lived and died an idiot.

Some time ago a correspondent sent me the following, clipped from some paper to me unknown. It relates to the performance of Haverley's Mastodon Minstrels, of which company, E. M. Hall, was at the time a member:

\*　　\*　　\*　　\*　　\*　　\*　　\*　　\*　　\*

"The only new features, were E. M. Hall, with his Banjo, and the Howe sextette, in place of the quartette of last season. Mr. Hall is one of the finest Banjo-players in the world, able to play much better music than he did last night, and we regret that he did not render some of the fine selections which have not only made him famous, but have elevated the musical status of the Banjo."

The fact is that no man who follows the minstrel business, and is compelled to "black up" from six to eight times per week, can always, upon every occasion, feel musically inclined, sufficiently to render with taste and expression, his best musical selections.

Then again, as has been previously stated, negro minstrelsy is a business which attracts persons of its own sphere, and not so many who care to hear really good music, as those who demand fun. Here you have the reasons why Mr. Hall does not always play his best selections.

I have said that there are some persons who do not know the difference between a Banjo and a tambourine. This is true. It is also true that there are others who do not know the difference between a Banjo and a guitar. The correspondent who wrote the following item was evidently of that kind ; for he, or she, recorded the teacher as having formed a class on the guitar, or in guitar playing, when indeed it was the Banjo and not the guitar.

The item referred to is from the *Quiz*, a society journal, and reads as follows :

" Mr. De Witt C. Everest, of Spruce street, has formed a class of pupils for instruction in the guitar, which is being ' taken up ' by society."

There was a " Banjo Tournament " held at Association Hall, Newburgh, N. Y., on Tuesday evening, May 24th, 1887. The following is a condensed report, clipped from a local paper :

" The tournament at Newburgh, Tuesday night, under the direction of Mr. W. B. Pethingale, was a great success. Every seat was sold, and standing-room was at a premium. Mr. Ruby Brooks, the finest Banjo-player in the world, gave great pleasure by his masterly handling of this popular instrument. Encore after encore was demanded, and obligingly responded to by Mr. Brooks. Mr. Webber accompanied him in his usual happy manner.

There was a large number of entries for the single and double classes. Representatives from Newburgh, Hudson, Poughkeepsie and Middletown gave exhibitions of every variety of Banjo-playing. The winners were as follows :

Hudson River championship for single, 1st prize, Mr. Vess Ossman, of Hudson.

2d prize, Mr. W. J. Connolly, of Poughkeepsie.

3d prize, Mr. Wm. H. Knapp, of Middletown.

Jas. Gemmill and Wm. Ross, of Poughkeepsie, won the double championship of the Hudson River."

I have never held a very high opinion of "Banjo tournaments." A tournament is supposed to represent a mock-fight, and is out of place among Banjo-players.

There are many excellent players of the Banjo, who would not have anything to do with a "contest,"—nor play for a prize of any description. Such contests merely decide the question,—if they decide anything at all,—of who was the best player upon a *certain occasion.* As it may happen, at any time, that a good performer does not feel in the humor for playing; or may find the surroundings and conditions not to his liking, nor in harmony with him he cannot play his best; whilst another, having less musical ability, but more "nerve," may carry off the prize. I think that playing for prizes is out of the range of a display of musical ability, and tends to excite combativeness and inharmony, which is not in keeping with true music. As advertisements,—used to attract attention to some particular make of Banjo,—such entertainments may be a success, but they have no place in art.

Fancy a number of violinists or pianists holding such a contest !

From *The Telegram,* [New York.]

## MR. REUBEN BROOKS THE EXTRAORDINARY BANJOIST OF THE DAY.

" Last evening a party of club-men met in the rooms of Mr. Reuben Brooks, on Broadway, to hear a little music and to enjoy themselves generally. It was the good fortune of a representative of the *Telegram* to be one of the party. We say the good fortune, for certainly a more extraordinary and satisfactory performance on an instrument has not been heard in this city by anybody. Mr. Brooks' execution on the Banjo last night was perfect. It was equal to anything ever done here by Remenyi, Wienawski or Wilhemi on their violins.

It has been the custom to regard roulades, vamps, beats with thimbles, and a series of florid chords, as the highest part of the art of Banjo-playing. Jigs, reels, marches, hornpipes, and now and then a simple gavotte were performed by ambitious members of minstrel and variety bands. Here and there in society was found an amateur who had the temerity and good taste to attempt something more than what were generally described as 'studies for the Banjo.' Even the best players, and the most skillful of those persons never could more than give the general idea of some of the most complicated of these themes, slurring over the difficulties, and hiding their own inability to accomplish positions, transpositions and harmonic pyrotechnics in rolls and florid runs which meant nothing, and, though ornate, were merely Banjo-tricks, and in no sense part of the score of the number being played. Last evening Mr. Brooks set at rest forever the question of the Banjo as an instrument for which all music could be written and arranged. He played " La Gitana," " The Funeral March of a Marionette," Auditi's famous gavotte, overtures to operas, operatic medleys, classical selections, waltzes and popular airs, and intricate numbers never attempted on any instrument except by the very greatest of artists. All of these things he played as they are written and harmonized; not a passage was faultily executed; not a chromatic run or chord of ' accidentals ' slighted or slurred; not a change of signatures altered for Banjo exigencies. Musicians who were auditors last night marvelled, and were delighted at his honesty, honor, fidelity and musical conscience. They could not comprehend his skill; they had never believed it possible for any man to do such work on the Banjo. They pronounced Mr. Reuben Brooks a veritable virtuoso, capable of playing on the Banjo any score that can be played upon the piano, or violin, or harp, and that they likewise declared Mr. Brooks to be as great in his line as Joseffy and others, who have been heard at Steinway Hall, heretofore, on the piano.

We have no hesitation in saying that his work was just as extraordinary in execution, and far more masterful and melodi-

ously harmonic, than Mr. Levy's on the cornet, and we are sure
that the future of this young artist will justify this statement.
Already he has been taken in hand and recognized by society
and the clubs, from which he derives a fine income both as a
teacher and a performer at private parties.

He is a thorough musician, and albeit only twenty-five years
old, discreet, modest, and entirely devoted to his art. He loves
his Banjo more than many men love their wives, and he has all
the intensity of purpose and incandescent enthusiasm which be-
get industry, perseverance and boundless success.

'Ruby' Brooks, as he is called by his friends, is not simply
a great artist, he is a wonder—the first man who ever really
made the Banjo the peer of the other great string instruments."

---

The foregoing article would be very good for the Banjo,
—were it not that it was evidently written by a person not
at all familiar with the Banjo, or its musical capabilities,
—and written entirely in the interests of one particular
individual.

Had the correspondent made himself familiar with the
Banjo and its players, previous to making the visit he
speaks of, to Mr. Brooks,—he would not have been so
liable to mistaken opinions, and so given to over-rate a
musical performance.

Mr. Brooks, it is true, is an excellent Banjo-player; but
there is nothing either wonderful or extraordinary about
his playing. What he does can be done by any young
man who possesses even an ordinary talent for music, and
the same application to practice which Mr. Brooks has
given to it.

More than this can be done by those who are willing
to stick at practice so continuously as to develop the
faculty to an abnormal extent; which, however, I do not
advise nor think advantageous. No wonder that those

individuals who have all along supposed the Banjo to be
a "tambourine with a handle," should open their eyes
and ears upon hearing a good Banjo in the hands of a
good player. What would such persons say upon hearing Weston at his best,—under the same conditions as
they heard Brooks, I wonder?

After an observation of some fifteen years, and an extended acquaintance with all the Banjo-players of note,
I must candidly say, in justice to the man with black
skin,—that nothing is done on a Banjo by any other man
that has not been done by him. The statements of those
who have not had an opportunity to hear him are of little
value here: I have heard them nearly all, and at their
best.

I know that there are some persons so deformed in
character, and so lacking in all sense of human feeling
and honorable principle,—that they would give no credit
whatever to a man who had not the same white skin as
their own,—no matter how great his abilities. Such persons will now possibly cast aside this volume with the
sneering remarks:—"Banjo! Nigger," etc., etc. But
curses, like chickens, "Come home to roost;" and such
remarks, have little effect.

## "VERA PRO GRATIIS."

(Truth before favor.)

## SECTION VI.

All manufacturers of Banjos and of most other musical instruments, are constantly coming in contact with persons who think they are competent to make improvements in the construction of musical instruments. Many and varied are the devices which have been suggested to me by zealous amateurs, for improving the Banjo, during my experience as a manufacturer.

Many persons experiment *blindly*, not possessing any theoretical knowledge of music or of the science of acoustics. Theoretical knowledge is a great help to any one who desires to experiment. Yet there are others,—persons of scientific attainments, who, through lack of talent, and being unable to enter fully in harmony with the subjects experimented upon, utterly fail in accomplishing anything.

Fetis, in his valuable work, *Music Explained to the World*, says: " All the distinguished men, who have employed themselves in the construction of instruments, have sought to make improvements in them, by a more severe application of theoretical principles; but, in practice, the results have not been such as they expected, either from unknown causes, or from their not having taken the necessary precautions.

*Theory is sometimes found in opposition to practice.* For example, the principles of the sounding of vibrating surfaces, demonstrates that violins, violas, and basses are constructed on arbitrary, rather than scientific rules; but in the application of these principles, no one has yet been able to make instruments as good as those which were made by rules, the foundation of which is unknown. The same thing may be remarked of pianos. Time alone will shed light on these mysterious circumstances."

———

These remarks fit the case of the Banjo. I was once asked the question why I did not secure the services of some distinguished expert—some professor of acoustics—some learned doctor of science, to assist me in improving the Banjo. Simply because I do not believe that such a person exists—I mean a learned professor, who, by applying his rules, could do anything for the Banjo. Such persons have done nothing for the violin, and it seems that I am not alone in my opinion upon this subject.

Where are the rules of science—and where are the scientific professors who can, by mathematical rules, explain to the painter just how he is to set to work to produce paintings of equal merit to those of the old Italian masters?

My theory upon this subject I have already given in my lecture, *The Banjo Philosophically*, and I have now to say that in the two years which have passed since I penned that article, I have found nothing to alter my opinion in any way, but many things to confirm and strengthen it.

There are many persons to whom a cheap chromo is as interesting as a fine painting; and such, I presume, do not care to learn anything about the superior qualities of the paintings of the old masters. There are likewise those to whom a cheap fiddle is as good as a fine violin; and others who are just as well pleased with a cheaply-made Banjo as with a finer instrument. Our art, however, does not depend, for its encouragement and support, upon persons of that character, and consequently I care little for either their censure or their praise. Where some of my

writings may be ridiculed and made the objects of adverse criticism by a certain class, I take it as part of the
lot of all who attempt to instruct ; and many such criticisms have just the weight of remarks sometimes passed
by servant-maids, or hotel waiters, upon the guests they
serve,—nothing more;—I am unaffected by reason of
them.

An interesting article pertaining to the manufacture of
bells, by the Rev. R. H. Haweis, in *Good Words*, contains the following :

\*    \*    \*    \*    \*    \*    \*

" A certain tact or rule of thought, takes the place of science;
rules there must be founded on principles, but the masters cannot explain their secrets. They produce the work of art; others
are left to discover the laws they have obeyed. When we have
analyzed their methods we may be able to make their bells. So
thought the Germans when they measured and analyzed Raphael
and Tintoret, and produced the correct but lifeless *banalites* of
Ary Scheffer; so thought Vuillaume when he imitated the very
wormholes in the Amatis; but for all that the French fiddles are
not Amatis. It may turn out that in the making of rich musical
bells like those of Van Aerschodt there is something which
cannot be taught—the instinct, the incommunicable touch."

Fetis says also, concerning the violin : " The violin
was for a long time only a vulgar instrument, confined
to the playing of popular airs and dances."

Just so it has been with the Banjo. But the violin has
now been so long recognized and established in public
favor that all this is overlooked or forgotten ; whilst with
the Banjo it is different.

I will now append what this celebrated writer says
concerning the guitar, as a musical instrument : *

* *Music Explained to the World*, page 252, American Edition.

"The limited resources of the guitar are well known. It seems calculated only to sustain the voice lightly in little vocal pieces, such as romances, couplets, boleros etc. Some artists, however, have not limited themselves to this small merit, but have sought to overcome the disadvantages of a meagre tone, the difficulties of the fingering, and the narrow compass of this instrument. Mr. Carulli was the first who undertook to perform difficult music on the guitar, and succeeded in it to such degree as to excite astonishment. Sor, Carcassi, Huerta, and Agnado, have carried the art to a higher degree of perfection; and if it were possible for the guitar to take a place in music, properly so-called, these artists would doubtless have effected that miracle; but to such a metamorphosis the obstacles are invincible."

Probably in musical works hereafter published, similiar views may be expressed upon our American Banjo. However, that is not of much moment.

Guitarists find to-day in the American Guitar-neck-Banjo,—a Banjo with neck like guitar,—an instrument of much greater power than the guitar; for which due credit must be given to the Banjo.

Let us now read a portion of what Moore, in his Encyclopædia of Music, has about the guitar:

"About the middle of the last century, the guitar was so fashionable in England as to threaten the ruin of those persons engaged in the manufacture of other instruments. The use of the guitar is said to have been stopped by Kirkman, a harpsichord maker. Having bought a number of cheap guitars, he gave them to ballad singers, and persons in the lowest sphere of life, teaching them at the same time how to play a few popular songs.* As soon as it became common, those who had been most interested in it as a fashionable toy, threw it by in disgust, and commenced again the study of the piano-forte.

Thus it is that fashion governs the inventions of the wisest,

---

* Mark the similarity between these and the "simple method" Banjo-players.

and consigns to neglect, or raises into estimation, the talents, genius, and industry of the greatest men in all ages and countries.

The demand for this beautiful and graceful instrument has of late so increased, that several American houses have commenced the manufacture of them.* The guitar seems to be coming into very general use."

I have never placed much dependence upon fashionable "society people" for the elevation of the Banjo. About all that can be said for fashion and its votaries is that it has drawn the attention of inquiring minds to the instrument.

Fashion is as fickle as she is lazy, and as vacillating as she is proud. Many such persons would like to play the Banjo because it is "the rage,"—but are too indolent to study and practice, and having no real love for the instrument never become players. The real development of the musical status of the Banjo lies entirely with those who have a natural affection for the instrument, and the ability to practice and study.

Such as "look down" upon the Banjo when it is a "plebeian" instrument, but take to it as soon as some fashionable nabob takes up with it, are not qualified by nature to become anything but mediocre performers upon it. "Flowers grow best for those who love them best." The Banjo is mastered only by those who, by reason of a natural love for it and its music, are in affinity with it.

Who among the real lovers of the guitar gave it up when fashion forsook it, as it is said to have done when an evil disposed and envious person attempted to drag it down? Probably not one, for it remains to this day as much loved by its devotees as ever. Harmony lives

* This was prior to the year 1854, when the Encyclopædia was published.

when discord and wrangling die. The fittest survive; and the fittest is always that which is in harmony with nature,—that which is most fit to exist.

---

Some persons may ask: Don't you think the Banjo will "go down,"—decline?

I most positively answer, no, I do not think it ever will; not, at least, until the earth is peopled with entire new races, and our people have become, like Atlantis, the lost continent, submerged in the mighty deep and forgotten. In the language of another, when speaking upon a different subject, I will say,—"It has, indeed, and may hereafter, be violently assaulted by delusive opinions; but the opposition will be just as imbecile as that of the waves of the sea against a temple built on a rock, which majestically pours them back,

' Broken and vanquished foaming to the main.' "

## "FINIS CORONAT OPUS."

## APPENDIX TO THIRD EDITION.

### THE BANJO UP TO DATE.

Now, that the great World's Columbian Exposition, held in Chicago, Illinois, in celebration of the 400th Anniversary of the Discovery of America, has come to a close, and the Banjo having been well represented and recognized as never before, and the Stewart Banjo having met with high honors, the author of " *The Banjo* " feels called upon to make some additions to the pages of his work, first published in 1888.

During the five years that has passed since the first edition of this little work was issued, so many and varied have been the notable events chronicled in the advance of the Banjo, as a musical instrument, that a complete review is out of the question at this time ; nevertheless, a brief summary of the most interesting and noticeable is herein given, together with a few practical remarks and suggestions deemed necessary in meeting the general demand.

Julian Hawthorne, the well known novelist, has seen fit, in one of his popular works, to speak of the Banjo as

" An instrument which has been much misrepresented and mis-made, as well as misused. There are nasal, metallic banjos, which are as exasperating as vulgar talkers. You can hear them a mile off, and the farther off the better. There are banjos which are mumbling and demoralized. But there are such things as good banjos, and the only instrument (made with hands) that equals a good banjo is a good violin ; but the violin must be heard alone, whereas a banjo is best when married to a sympathetic human voice.

Its strings seem to be the very chords of being; their music is so near to life, that they seem to vibrate from the emotions of the player. The sounds are mellow; in their essence they are pathetic, though they can rise to a humorous cheerfulness, as one laughs with a sorrow at the heart. It is the music of nature, ordered and humanized. No charlatan or coarse minded person can play on such a banjo; it is a fatal revealer of character. Passionate and gentle natures use the instrument best, and men oftener than women."

The above beautifully expressed tribute to the Banjo I am glad to give space to, wishing to place Mr. Hawthorne on record in the "Banjo World." No doubt banjoists of the day will ever have a warm place in their hearts for this writer, although many may disagree with him in the statement that "a Banjo is best when married to a sympathetic human voice,"—the solo performance of classical music upon the Banjo, recently introduced by the gifted young artist, Alfred A. Farland, having done much to convince them that the Banjo finds its true sphere as a solo instrument—*not as an accompaniment.*

During the last five years the Banjo has made rapid strides in popularity, and great progress has been made in its management, both in solo work and in combination with the guitar, mandolin, etc.

Banjo Clubs,—organizations composed of five, six, or more banjos,—have multiplied until we now have such organizations in all of our principal cities. The manner of organization, arrangement of music and improvement in instrumentation is also greatly marked.

With the advent of the "Banjeaurine" came the permanent Banjo organization.

The Piccolo Banjo, Guitar-neck Banjo, Six String Accompaniment Banjo, and Bass Banjo were added one by one, and gradually the sphere of Banjo music enlarged, as the combination of instruments improved.

Thomas J. Armstrong, of Philadelphia, the talented composer and teacher of Banjo music, gave much of his time to the study of the instrument and its utilization in orchestral combinations; the result being a work on "Banjo Orchestra Music," containing many examples in musical arrangements of this kind, and many useful hints to leaders and organizers of Banjo clubs.

This was the first and only work produced which placed the information directly in the hands of the organizer of a Banjo Club, enabling him to successfully organize a combination of Banjos and arrange music adapted to it. The same author is at the present time engaged in completing a far more important work, called "Divided Accompaniment," which is being serially published in the Banjo and Guitar *Journal*, and which, when completed, will appear in book form. "Divided Accompaniment" is looked upon as a step in advance of the present status of the Banjo organization, and its adoption in all large and well organized Banjo and Guitar Clubs ·is made possible by the use of the Bass Banjo, an instrument, which, though it may be liable to misuse, is as important to the Banjo organization, as the double bass to the orthodox orchestra.

For the encouragement of Banjo Clubs, a series of annual entertainments was begun in Philadelphia, in the shape of "Contests" between different Banjo and Guitar organizations for prizes, the first entertainment of the kind coming off at Association Hall, in January of 1892.

So great was the success of the first entertainment of this series that it was found necessary to secure a larger hall for the second event, which took place in the American Academy of Music, on Saturday evening, January 14th, 1893,—every seat having been sold before the doors opened for the concert, and the house being crowded in every part with a most enthusiastic audience. On this occasion there were ten instruments awarded as prizes to ten competing Clubs.

The first prize, consisting of a Stewart "Presentation Banjo," valued at $125.00, was awarded to the Hamilton Club, a Philadelphia organization, under the able leadership of Mr. Paul Eno, the gentlemanly teacher and performer.

The Hamilton Banjo, Mandolin and Guitar Clubs also won the leading prizes at the entertainment of the previous year, and are consequently looked upon as very strong and well drilled organizations. The success of the Hamiltons spread the fame of Mr. Eno as an organizer and teacher of Banjo, Mandolin and Guitar Clubs to such an extent, that his services were soon in great demand, until he now has many Clubs under his instruction.

Thus has the interest in Banjo organizations been stimulated and the status improved, until the Banjo Club is now a recognized musical feature in all first-class entertainments.

It may not be deemed out of place to give here the programme of the second annual event spoken of, which was as follows :

1. " Normandie March "—*Armstrong* } Armstrong's Banjo Orchestra
   " Martaneaux Overture "—*Vernet* }         (125 performers).

2. Vocal Selections, . . . . . . . . . . . . . . . Master Lem. Stewart

3. Banjo Solo—" Yorktown Polka " . . . . . . . . . . . . . *Buckley*.
   Master Fred. Stewart.

4. Banjo Solo —" Old Folks at Home," (with variations) . . . *Foster*.
   Miss E. E. Secor.

5. Banjo Solo—" Modjeska Waltzes " . . . . . . . . . . . *Lowthain*.
   S. S. Stewart.

6. A Few Moments with Bolsover Gibbs.

7. *a.* Spanish Dances, Nos. 1, 2 and 3 . . . . . . . . . *Moszkowski*.
   *b.* Concerto, Allegro molto vivace, op. 64 . . . . . . *Mendelssohn*.
   Alfred A. Farland, the scientific Banjoist, of Pittsburg, Pa.

The following Clubs competed for the prizes:

1. "Corcoran Cadet March" . . . . . . . . . . . . . . . . . . . *Sousa.*
   The Hamilton Banjo Club, Paul Eno, Leader.

2. "Gladiator March" . . . . . . . . . . . . . . . . . . . . *Sousa.*
   The American Students, J. H. Minges, Leader.

3. "The Bugle Call" . . . . . . . . . . . . . . . . . . . . *Folwell.*
   The Camden Banjo Club, John C. Folwell, Leader.

4. "March, The Dandy Fifth" . . . . . . . . . . . . . . . *Farland.*
   The Carleton Banjo Club, Henry Howison, Leader.

5. "Bouquet Polka" . . . . . . . . . . . . . . . . . . . . *Havese.*
   The University of Penna. Banjo Club, Paul Eno, Leader.

6. "Imperial Grand March" . . . . . . . . . . . . . . . *Jennings.*
   The Alma Banjo Club, of Williamsport, H. G. Molson, Leader.

7. "Mocking Bird with Var's" . . . . . . . . . . . . . . *Winner.*
   The Philomela Sextette, Edw. Frueh, Leader.

8. Waltz—"La Serenata" . . . . . . . . . . . . . . . . . *Jaxone.*
   The Hamilton Mandolin and Guitar Club, Paul Eno, Leader.

9. "World's Fair Medley" . . . . . . . . . . . . . . . . .
   The International Serenaders, O. H. Albrecht, Leader.

10. "Red Cross Gavotte" . . . . . . . . . . . . . . . . . *Bellano.*
    The Castilian Troubadours, A. F. Bellano, Leader.

Final—Judges' Decisions and the Awarding of Prizes to the Clubs.

The third Concert of the series, which came off at the Academy of Music, on Saturday Evening, January 13th, last, (1894) was even more exciting than that of the previous year.

The following account of the event appeared in the Banjo and Guitar *Journal,* issued February 1st, (Number 80).

"The Third Annual Banjo Club Contest for Prizes, in Philadelphia, came off at the Academy of Music, Broad and Locust Sts., on Saturday Evening, January 13, with one of the largest audiences ever assembled in the Academy.

The following program was rendered :

1. Grand Banjo Orchestra,          Thos. J..Armstrong Conductor.
   a. Amphion March—*Stewart.*    b. Martaneaux Overture—*Vernet.*
2. Master Lem Stewart in Vocal Selections.
   (Miss Florence Schmidt, Accompanist.)
3. Banjo Solo.
   *Sonata op. 30* { a. Allegro Assai.   b. Moderato. } *Beethoven.*
                  {      c. Allegro Vivace.    }
   Alfred A. Farland—Miss Annie Farland, Accompanist.
4. The Gregory Trio.
   a. Grand March from Tannhaeuser . . . . . . . . . . *Wagner*
   b. Violette Waltzes . . . . . . . . . . . . . . . . *Waldteufel*
            Geo. W. Gregory, W. B. Farmer, *Banjoists,*
            Chas. Van Baar, *Pianist.*

The following Clubs played in competition for the Prizes :

BANJO CLUB CLASS.

1. Portland Overture . . . . . . . . . . . . . . . . . . . . . . *Folwell*
            Camden Banjo Club, John C. Folwell, Leader.
2. La Czarina, Mazourka Russe . . . . . . . . . . . . . . . *Ganne*
            Hamilton Banjo Club, Paul Eno, Leader.
3. "Dandy Fifth" Quick Step . . . . . . . . . . . . . . . *Farland*
            Carleton Banjo Club, M. Rudy Heller, Leader.
4. Vendome Galop . . . . . . . . . . . . . . . . . . . . . . *Armstrong*
            Alma Banjo Club, (of Williamsport) Jas. S. Purdy, Leader.
5. Cocoanut Dance . . . . . . . . . . . . . . . . . . . . . . *Hermann*
            Lehigh University Banjo Club, C. E. Pettinos, Leader.
6. Southern Jollification, Medley . . . . . . . . . . . . . *arr. Eno*
            University of Penna. Banjo Club, Paul Eno, Leader.
7. La Felice Waltz . . . . . . . . . . . . . . . . . . . . . *Eno*
            Century Wheelmen Banjo Club, F. H. Garrigues, Leader.
8. Bella Bocca Polka . . . . . . . . . . . . . . . . . . . . *Waldteufel*
            Drexel Institute Banjo Club, Mahlon Rattay, Leader.

MANDOLIN CLUB CLASS.

1. March Cyclorama . . . . . . . . . . . . . . . . . . . . . *Belano*
            The American Students, J. H. Minges, Leader.
2. Alvin March . . . . . . . . . . . . . . . . . . . . . . . . *Sanford*
            The Philomela Mandolin, Guitar and Banjo Orchestra,
            Edward Fruch, Leader.
3. "Simple Confessions" . . . . . . . . . . . . . . . . . . *Thome*
            Hamilton Mandolin Club, Paul Eno, Leader.
4. Selections from Il Trovatore . . . . . . . . . . . . . . *arr. Belano*
            Fleischhauer's Philadelphia Mandolin Club,
            H. Fleischhauer, Leader.

For those not familiar with the list of prizes and manner of awarding same to competing clubs, we give the following: The competition was divided into two distinct classes: First, the Banjo Club Class, composed of Clubs using Banjos as leading instruments, and generally known as Banjo Clubs. Second, Mandolin Club Class, composed of Mandolin Clubs; such organizations as used Mandolins for leading parts.

The Banjo Clubs and Mandolin Clubs were not in competition with each other.

The Judges, three in number, were Sep. Winner, the well-known composer; S. H. Kendle, leader of First Regiment Band, and Frank M. Stevens, of the New York *Musical Courier*.

There were eight Banjo Prizes for the Banjo Clubs, and four prizes for the Mandolin Clubs, as follows:

### BANJO CLUBS.

|  | Valued at |
|---|---|
| *First*—Stewart's World's Fair Prize Banjo and Case | $250 00 |
| *Second*—Handsomely Inlaid Stewart Banjo and Case from World's Fair | 150.00 |
| *Third*—Stewart Banjo and Case | 75.00 |
| *Fourth*—Stewart "Orchestra" Banjo and Case | 60.00 |
| *Fifth*—Stewart "Champion" Banjo and Case | 50.00 |
| *Sixth*—Stewart "Thoroughbred" Banjo and Case | 46.00 |
| *Seventh*—Stewart "Banjeaurine" and Case | 36.00 |
| *Eighth*—Stewart "Piccolo" Banjo and Case | 25.00 |

### MANDOLIN CLUBS.

|  | Valued at |
|---|---|
| *First*—Geo. Bauer Mandolin and Case | $100.00 |
| *Second*—Concert Guitar and Case | 50.00 |
| *Third*—Weymann & Son Mandolin and Case | 35.00 |
| *Fourth*—Weymann & Son Guitar and Case | 25 00 |

The First Prize in the latter named class was contributed by George Bauer, manufacturer of high class mandolins, whose office is 1224 Chestnut Street, where those interested can write for catalogues.

The Second Prize in the Mandolin Class, was a beautiful concert guitar, presented by Robert C. Kretschmar, No. 136 North Ninth Street.

The Third and Fourth Prizes in this class were kindly contributed by Weymann & Son, manufacturers, No. 45 North Ninth Street, and are known as the "Keystone State Mandolins and Guitars."

The First and Second Banjo Prizes were the two handsomest Stewart Banjos exhibited at the Chicago World's Fair.

The three Judges made their points on *Harmony, Expression* and *General Excellence*, and the combined averages formed the basis upon which the prizes were awarded. The managers of the concert had nothing whatever to do with the awards, and, in fact, held no conversation with the Judges upon the subject—the matter being left entirely to their unbiased musical opinions.

Their decision placed the awards as follows:

### BANJO CLUBS.

*First Prize*—Carleton Banjo Club . . . . . . . . . . . . 12 members
*Second Prize*—Century Wheelmen Banjo Club . . . . . 15 "
*Third Prize*—Drexel Institute Banjo Club . . . . . . . 8 "
*Fourth Prize*—Camden Banjo Club . . . . . . . . . . . 6 "
*Fifth Prize*—Hamilton Banjo Club . . . . . . . . . . . 18 "
*Sixth Prize*—Lehigh University Banjo Club . . . . . . 14 "
*Seventh Prize*—University of Pennsylvania Banjo Club 17 "
*Eighth Prize*—Alma Banjo Club . . . . . . . . . . . . 8 "

### MANDOLIN CLUBS.

*First Prize*—American Students Mandolin Club . . . . 5 members
*Second Prize*—Hamilton Mandolin Club . . . . . . . . 15 "
*Third Prize*—Fleischhauer's Phila. Mandolin Club . . 19 "
*Fourth Prize*—Philomela Mandolin Club . . . . . . . . 11 "

Everything pertaining to the concert was a grand success, with the exception of the *finale*—that is, the awards of prizes by the Judges; this, of course, can never be wholly satisfactory."

There is no doubt that Banjo organizations have been greatly improved since the first Prize Concert, of January, '92, the competitive exhibitions having proved a stimulus, but as the awards must depend always upon the opinions of three (or possibly five) men, acting in the capacity of judges, there is little reason for believing the result of such contests can ever be satisfactory to all interested parties.

The "Banjo Orchestra," under the direction of Mr. Armstrong, was composed of Banjeaurines, Banjos, Mandolins and Guitars, assisted by 'cellos and double bass ; the ladies and gentlemen, one hundred and twenty-five in all, presenting a pleasing sight as the curtain rose. There had been several organizations of similar character presented at former Banjo concerts in New York and Boston, but none, it is believed, so well drilled and balanced as this. Counterpoint and the laws of harmony had been conscientiously observed by Mr. Armstrong, the able conductor, and the *lights and shades of musical expression* were particularly noticeable and commented upon by musicians in the audience.

It is no easy task to assemble and drill an organization of this kind ; but its complete success, musically, amply repaid its talented and painstaking conductor.

It becomes a necessary though painful duty to chronicle here the death of Horace Weston, the famous colored banjoist, who departed this life in the city of New York, on May 22d, 1890, at the age of sixty-five years.

Weston, though colored, was musically endowed to a high degree, and at times produced most wonderful and weird music from the Banjo. He was the first artist to adopt the Stewart Banjo, and through his masterly performances in all of our principal cities throughout the country, attracted universal attention to this instrument.

It is not always the pioneer, however, who reaches the topmost round of the ladder in his particular art, and the wonderful performances of Weston—as surprising as they were at the time—did not embrace the marvelous rendition of classical music, such as is now being rendered by such artists as Alfred A. Farland.

Weston was, in the opinion of the writer, the most original and wonderful performer of his time, and now that he will be heard no more, it is well that the memory of his genius be chronicled here and handed down to posterity, for although of the African race, he was a genius indeed.

The death of a most gifted and painstaking writer and composer, which took place in San Diego, California, on September 7th, 1890, it is also a painful duty to record. The departure from this life of John H. Lee is here referred to. Truly a gifted musician and one having the interests of the Banjo at heart.

Long may he live in the musical compositions left behind. Those who knew him best respected him most, and those familiar with the work he did in elevating the status of the Banjo, can never forget him.

Others have come forth to astonish us with their musical powers displayed upon the Banjo. Its development has continued. It is no longer the instrument of the negro minstrel entertainer, nor the symbol of grotesque fantasm. *Its Apotheosis has taken place.*

## THE APOTHEOSIS OF THE BANJO.

Alfred A. Farland, "the man who plays concertos and sonatas upon the Banjo," came forth as a shining light, as it were, out of the darkness.

Coming to Philadelphia, from his home in Pittsburg, in January, 1893, to take his position as the soloist of the evening, his rendition upon the Banjo of *Mendelssohn's Concerto, Allegro, molto vivace*, opus 64, was at once a surprise and a revelation. Musicians of taste and culture among the audience—some of whom perhaps had "never thought much of a Banjo" up to this time—were surprised and astonished. A new and higher sphere seemed to envelop the instrument. It was no longer an instrument of purely *staccato tone*, all the sustained sounds found in the original violin solo being produced with telling effect and beautiful expression by Mr. Farland, from the Banjo. Few indeed would have believed it possible. This young artist since that time has continued perseveringly onward, meeting with complete success as a banjoist in circles where the Banjo had not heretofore received just recognition.

On October 16th, of last year, our young artist was called to Jersey City, N. J., to take part in a Concert of the Jersey City Banjo Club, given in the Tabernacle of that city. His triumph there,—he being an entire stranger in the city and to the audience assembled,—I cannot but look upon as a giant step of progress for our favorite instrument.

The following review of the concert, from the *Evening Journal*, should be read by all. It will be noticed that all I have ever claimed for the possibilities of the Banjo, and perhaps all that has ever been predicted of its future, is now acknowledged as fulfilled.

"Time was when the Banjo was regarded as a barbaric instrument, fit only to be picked by semi-savage fingers. The legend has it that Ham, the first 'nigger,' becoming lonely in the ark, made a banjo with strings of opossum hair, and 'knocked out' tunes to the intense delight of the rest of the family. Many of us can remember how, in the palmy days of Bryant's, and Christy's and Wood's, and the San Francisco Minstrels, the banjo, in the hands of some grotesquely attired fellow was quite a feature. Then we saw it rise gradually until there were champion banjo players, who proudly handled silver-plated instruments, and dressed in silken doublet and hose. Even that step in advance did not remove the banjo from the lowly position it had occupied for ages. All this is different now. The banjo has become a classical instrument. Its apotheosis has taken place, and Jersey City was last night treated to a remarkable exhibition of the apotheosized banjo. It was at a concert given by the Jersey City Banjo Club. The Tabernacle was crowded in every part, and never did a more enthusiastic crowd meet in that great meeting place.

The banjo club took the first number. The club is composed of Prof. Robert Wood, Charles Bammesberger, Fred. Clark, Frank Mullins and Master Nelson Vanderhoof. Said the program: 'The Jersey City Banjo Club is a comparatively new organization and owes its inception to Prof. Robert Wood, through whose efforts the club was organized not quite two years ago. The young men who compose it were all pupils of Prof. Wood, and their sole object in thus banding themselves together was that of mutual improvement. The idea that they would ever appear in public and at large concerts never entered their heads, but appreciative admirers drew them out from their retirement and in a short time they were in such demand that offers of engagements were received from every side. They appeared at a number of entertainments in this city last winter and their excellent rendition of classic and popular music won for them many encomiums. They played ' Love and Beauty Waltzes' in fine style and responded to enthusiastic recalls. Their work was excellent. Mr. W. W. Baxter, the able manager of the entertainment, had done what had never before been accomplished. He had brought together the greatest banjo players of this country. The first of these to appear was Mr. Alfred A. Farland, of Pittsburg, Pa. He has been spoken of as the ' Paderewski of the banjo.' His playing was the very apotheosis of the instrument. Just imagine Beethoven's Sonata, op.

30, with Allegro Assai, Moderato and Allegro Vivace movements, played upon a banjo, and so played that all their exquisite parts were brought out in such perfection that a thousand people hung upon the sweet sounds with breathless interest and delight! That is what happened last night. It was wonderful.

The people who heard his great performance last night went wild with delight and recalled him again and again. The next brilliant feature was the playing of the Gregory Trio, composed of Messrs. G. W. Gregory, W. B. Farmer, banjoists, and Charles Van Baar, pianist. Their style is very different from that of Mr. Farland, but it is very interesting. They were compelled to respond to several encores, and delighted the audience immensely. Another banjo star is Mr. William George Rush. He affects high ballad and classical music, with wonderful arpeggios and harmonies, variations and chords. He played the 'Miserere' and 'Palms' and the audience rose at him—literally rose at him. He was compelled to respond to four encores. Messrs. Brooks and Denton were the remaining stars. They played waltzes and marches and proved themselves adepts. Mr. Farland closed his efforts with a great rendition of the overture to 'William Tell.' We omitted to mention that the Gregory Trio played as their set pieces the 'Intermezzo from Cavalleria Rusticana' and a march by Mr. Gregory."

Such a performance as Mr. Farland renders upon the Banjo cannot be heard at a minstrel or variety show for it does not come within the sphere of such, the mental status of the two conditions being separated by a wide gulf.

Geo. W. Gregory, the performer spoken of in connection with the "Gregory Trio," is an artist of great power and skill. He has a wonderful execution upon the Banjo, and, being a thoroughly capable musician, his arrangements for his Trio, consisting of two banjos and piano, are superior to the general run. One of Mr. Gregory's recent musical compositions for the Banjo, the L'Infanta

March, has met with very great success, displaying the composer's ability and originality. The difficulties overcome by the composer in the execution of this March has proven a revelation to many so-called banjoists.

The powerful tone produced by this artist, together with his wonderful dexterity of fingering, have combined to place him in a very high position among the "Banjo lights" of the present day.

As an instructor, Mr. Gregory is at the present time meeting with much success, and his "School for the Banjo" in New York City, where the Banjo and Musical Science is taught, bids fair to rival the celebrated musical schools of Europe. Truly, indeed, is the Banjo making its way to the topmost rounds of the ladder of musical position.

## DIFFICULTIES.

There have been, and there still remain, many obstacles to overcome in the successful use of the banjo upon all occasions. But as it is not by floating with the tide, but by contending against it, that manhood is developed, so it is and has been with the progress of our instrument.

Dampness is averse to a clear musical tone at all times and with all instruments. Particularly is this applicable to a banjo, for, while it suffers from the effect of moisture, as all other stringed instruments, and perhaps to an extreme degree, on account of the severe tension and severe handling of its strings, it must suffer more than any other instrument through the effect of atmospheric changes upon its sensitive sounding-board, the calfskin head. The recognition of this has led to much experiment with a view to overcoming at least part of the difficulty, and the constant contending with such obstacles has led to a much better understanding of the peculiarities of the instrument and the conditions essential to securing the best possible musical results. There is, indeed, little use of attempting to rank as a "soloist," unless the performer thoroughly understands his instrument, and is competent to maintain it in the best playing condition.

Recently, in enlarging my well-known work, "*The Complete American Banjo School*," considerable space was given to the discussion of the Banjo head, strings, etc., and as the work now stands, more information on these subjects is placed before the student than ever before.

A few remarks, however, may be here in order.

## BANJO HEADS.

The Banjo head, from the nature of the material of which it is made, must be very sensitive and easily affected by changes of weather.

Heat, or dry, cool weather contracts the head. Dampness, or moist weather, causes the head to relax.

These opposite effects are always produced, modified by existing conditions.

Experienced performers know that heads vary in quality fully as much as strings, and as both articles are made from animal material this is quite natural.

The skins from which Banjo heads are manufactured are obtained from several of our States, and their quality and nature vary greatly, and require different modes of treatment in order to secure good results.

Even when the head manufacturer obtains the right grade of skins, he is dependent in a great measure upon atmospheric conditions for his result.

The best heads are always made during the summer season, and when stock made at that season has become exhausted, and heads that are finished during cold weather must be used, there is constant trouble with breaking, and the banjo maker's lot is not a happy one.

Amateurs will be puzzled to know why it is that a head bearing a certain maker's name will give such good satisfaction at one time, and the heads from the same maker break so easily at another time. The main reason is that the heads were made at different seasons of the year. Other causes may be in inferior skins, or in mistakes made by workmen during the process of manufacture.

In stretching the head on the banjo rim, the performer may overstep the mark,—go a little too far in straining,—and by such error of judgment put an end to the life of an otherwise good head.

Suppose a performer stretches a new head upon his instrument, and after having everything apparently right and to his satisfaction, starts out to play at an entertainment. Finding the dressing room damp, he discovers the head becoming slack. Now, he is anxious to appear to the best advantage, and begins, with his wrench, to "pull down the head" again so as to have it tight.

We will suppose that he duly gives his performance and all goes well. Perhaps an evening or so later he repeats the same operation at another concert Finally, after several strainings of the kind described, he meets with a hall or room where the atmosphere is dry and warm, or it may turn out to be a very cold evening, and an intensely hot fire is kept up within doors. The head is then caused to contract and become intensely firm and tight. Perhaps it snaps at once. Perhaps it possesses exceptional powers of endurance, and lives through this attack of contraction. However the case may be, it can not stand a great deal more of that kind of treatment and must soon give way. Those brilliant performers who nearly always have their banjos in brilliant condition regardless of the weather, use up a great many heads.

Some performers make a practice of stretching two or three heads on a banjo rim, then removing one after another and keeping them on hand, ready shaped to the rim, and with the flesh hoops left in them. It is then possible to replace a head, if necessary, an hour or two before a concert. But such practice is considerable of a trouble and cannot always be depended upon, for the head put on dry and hard is apt to be very short-lived.

It is not unusual to meet with ambitious banjoists who claim to have invented a certain method for getting all the stretch out of a head before it is put on the Banjo, so that the head will remain as tight in wet weather as in dry.

I have, however, never as yet seen any evidence of such a result having been reached. It certainly appears that a very great difference exists in heads. There are exceptionally good ones, that require little stretching and resist dampness to a marked degree. But the majority of heads are not so accommodating. It would seem in the very nature of the case that if an ordinary head were strained so that it remained hard and tense in damp weather, it must likewise possess the opposite virtue; for otherwise such a head must also lack all power of contraction. If moisture cannot expand the fibres, or hot, dry air contract them, the head cannot possess those sensitive qualities so necessary to the purposes it is intended for.

The Rogers, celebrated head manufacturers, know a great deal about Banjo heads, and they have assured me that they have never yet been able to produce any such result. To use Mr. Rogers' own words, he says:—"We have not discovered anything to take the stretch out of some heads. Some will stretch until they break." Figuratively speaking, "we cannot have our penny and our cake, too." We cannot very well have winter and summer on the same day, as Christmas and the Fourth of July won't mix.

Therefore, if we expect to retain those indispensable musical qualities found in the calfskin head, we must be willing to put up with some of the disadvantages possessed by it also.

When good fortune gives us heads of extra fine quality we should endeavor to use them well, and not "wear out the welcome" by overstraining or abuse.

As time goes on, no doubt the process of head manufacture will be improved, in keeping with other improvements, and when the time comes that a perfect forecast of atmospheric conditions is possible, the head makers will be enabled to carry on the open air work only at favorable times. It is this unfavorable weather coming on unexpectedly, that is the greatest impediment to the manufacture of reliable Banjo heads, as well as of gut strings.

## THE FRETTED BANJO.

It is, perhaps, unnecessary to tell the Banjoist of the day that the raised fret fingerboard has become the thing in universal use. There are now so few Banjoists who use the old style smooth fingerboard Banjo, in this country, that Banjos are now made with raised frets almost entirely—the smooth board, with "dot frets," once styled "professional frets"—now being furnished by manufacturers only to order.

After some experiments in the direction of securing the best thing in the line of frets, the writer finally adopted a wire for the purpose, of about one-half the size of that in general use, and the Stewart Banjos made during the past four years have been fretted with this improved small fretting wire.

The execution of the left hand has been found much easier, and more accurate with this fretting, and, in an otherwise good instrument, that disagreeable "clanky" tone, which usually accompanies the old style frets, is not found when the narrow frets are used.

Mr. Farland, in his wonderful performances of violin concertos and other classical music, found the Stewart Banjo with the small raised frets best adapted to the purpose. And now that an almost perfect fretting scale is used, together with improved mechanical appliances for the work, the small raised fret has become almost a positive fixture with all good Banjos.

A more lengthy and elaborate article upon this subject may be found in the writer's *American Banjo School*, to which our readers are referred, should they desire to become more fully informed upon the subject.

## "CONCERT PITCH."

The "ordinary Banjo" of the present day is tuned to the pitch of C—that is, the third string of the instrument being tuned to G, gives C for the bass string. This pitch is pretty generally used among Banjo organizations at the present time. The Banjeaurines or Tenor Banjos are tuned a fourth above this pitch, and the Piccolo Banjos a full octave above.

The pitch of C, too, is generally considered the solo concert pitch, for Banjos not smaller than eleven inch rim, with nineteen inch fingerboard. As this tuning pitch readily admits of the bass string being raised,—"Tuned to B" as it is termed,—it is not likely that a higher pitch will ever become generally adopted. It is well, however, to caution the young performer against the use of too thin strings, for a good tone with strings that are too light, cannot possibly be obtained at this pitch.

A great many brilliant concert performers have adopted the pitch of A as the standard for the third string. This brings the bass string to D, and by the increased pressure of the strings upon the bridge and the increased tension, produces a much greater volume of tone. Of course, the strings at this pitch, on a Banjo of the size used by Mr. Gregory, must be very tense and difficult to manipulate. Then, too, it is impossible to raise the "Bass to B,"—which, however, is something that is never done by some of our leading soloists,—there being no bass strings in the world that would stand such harsh treatment. In some organizations, where Guitars of extra large size are used, it is deemed wise to tune the Banjo a half-tone lower than the accustomed C pitch, for the reason that the oversized Guitars will not stand well at concert pitch, and must be tuned a half-tone flat.

This is a rather poor policy, as it places the Banjo at a disadvantage, and deprives it of much of its brilliancy.

The average amateur banjoist can scarcely be expected to harden his fingers to the use of the extra high pitch banjo—such as the 12-inch rim Banjo, "tuned to D"— as used by Mr. Gregory, whose fingers are like steel, and retain their hardness even through the summer months, being kept in condition by several hours daily practice, together with a half hour or so on the guitar, in order to harden such portions of the finger-ends as are not well done up by Banjo practice alone.

## MAKE NO MISTAKE.

A well strained and tight head, together with well regulated strings and a proper tuning, are indispensable adjuncts to a good Banjo ; but it by no means follows that a poor Banjo will be transformed into a good one, by any changes possible to its head or strings. Experienced banjoists are well aware of this.

A Banjo that possesses a poor tone may be stimulated, as it were, by tightening the head and raising the pitch of its strings, but such proceeding will not make a good Banjo out of a poor one. Yet there are a great many instruments sold to inexperienced players in this way. A good instrument has the head slackened, or left without proper stretching, is strung with inferior strings and used for the purpose of showing off the superiority (?) of some cheaply made instrument, which of course is shown with good strings and a well regulated head.

The inexperienced buyer who draws his conclusions from "first appearences" is often deceived.

The fact that broken-down horses are often doctored up and shown to advantage on the tanbark or soft roads, and disposed of to unitiated buyers, is notórious. And the same thing is done with pianos, and, on a smaller scale, with Banjos. Up to within a very few years, there were few banjoists who really knew the requisite qualifications of a good Banjo. As no such music as Mr. Farland performs to-day on his Stewart Banjo, was ever attempted a few years ago, the requirements in a good Banjo were not so exacting.

A "sharp tone" on the "open strings" alone, will not make a Banjo "pass muster", to-day, as a good instrument. Banjoists are becoming educated, as the possibilities of the instrument become better recognized.

## STRINGS.

Wire strings, however applicable they be to the mandolin or zither, are entirely out of place upon a Banjo,
where the finger-ends must be used to set the strings in
vibration. The best of all strings are the old-fashioned
gut, which are produced from the intestines of young
lambs. Gut strings are flexible and musical. They
possess, however, two distinct disadvantages—liability
to break readily during damp or murky weather, and
falseness in tone through uneven finish. (See page 63).

During the last three or four years, experiments have
been made with a view to producing banjo strings of
silk, the fibres of which are prepared by boiling or steep-
ing in a gelatinous preparation, evidently a glue produced from material of the same nature as that which
composes the gut string.

Some of these strings, particularly those made of
*twisted* silk, possess a very brilliant tone, and on account
of being evenly spun, it is unusual to find a *false* string
among them. The difficulty is, however, that the string
of twisted silk, although very strong and durable in resisting tension, will not withstand a sharp bend or knot,
and for this reason breaks readily at the peg or tail-
piece. It is necessary to moisten the end of such strings
in knotting at the tail piece, which has a tendency to
prevent the string breaking off at the knot, but as the
string cannot be treated in this manner at the peg very
readily, it is doubtful if the twisted silk string will ever
become a complete success. They are *true* in tone and
quite brilliant, and are not affected to any great extent
by dampness, but they break readily from other causes,
as shown.

Of the silk strings of recent manufacture that are not
twisted, (the smooth silk string), there is this to be said :

Great improvement is shown in their manufacture, and the best makes of these strings do not break where tied or knotted, and are true in tone and even in finish. They are very strong and possess a brilliant tone and are not so liable to break through changes in temperature as gut strings. The only impediment to the use of the smooth silk strings appears to lie in the fact of their becoming slightly "fuzzy," after being used for a short time, where pressed upon the frets, making them short lived.

Those who may have attempted the use of "silk strings," and "given up in disgust" after the first trial, need not feel discouraged. There is more than one kind of silk string now being made, and the product of the different manufacturers varies as greatly as the product of different manufacturers in other lines.

I look for the final perfection of the silk string, and believe that within a few years it will supersede the old-fashioned gut string, which must ever vary with our changeable climate. Looking upon the progress already made in this branch of art since the subject was brought to notice * in the former editions of this work, it seems that three or four years more should give us the silk string *par excellence*.

As regards the Banjo tail-piece, to which the strings are attached, there are a great many different kinds now on the market, and new inventions in that line appear to be going in and out of the Patent Office constantly. People will keep on inventing one thing and another and taking out patents as long as human nature exists. The fact remains, however, that the Banjo Tail-pieces which are not "patented" remain superior to any of the clap-trap patents in that line.

Mr. Gregory, the great player, of New York, who as stated, tunes his Stewart Banjos to an extremely high

---

* See article on Strings, beginning on page 63.

pitch, finds that for this purpose there is nothing like the old-fashioned wooden tail-piece, which he fastens to the instruments with a double thickness of gut. Experience has confirmed his experiments, he says, convincing him that strings will not break so readily with this tail-piece.

One objection, however, to the use of the old-fashioned tail-piece for general purposes, is the trouble the amateur would be forced to encounter in the constant changing and adjusting of the gut fastening, which must be altered as the hoop is drawn down with the stretching of the head. This difficulty is not encountered by Mr. Gregory, owing to the fact that he stretches all heads over an additional rim before using them, and therefore is never obliged to use an instrument with the edge of the hoop up above the surface of the head.

Our little "Common-sense" tail-piece, now used by hundreds of public performers, seems also to give good satisfaction—there is no patent right attached to it, however, and the writer is quite sure that it answers all purposes and meets the requirements of most players.

# CONTENTS.

————:0:————

---

**EDITH E. SECOR.**

ADA G. McCLELLAND.

THOS. J. ARMSTRONG.

META B. HENNING.

**WILLIAM A. HUNTLEY.**

**JOHN H. LEE.**

**G. L. LANSING.**

J. E. HENNING.

# S. S. Stewart's Banjo and Guitar ➤ Journal

Published every other month

Six times a year

by S. S. Stewart, Philadelphia, Pa.

## PRICE, 10 CENTS PER COPY
## SUBSCRIPTION, 50 CENTS PER YEAR
PAYABLE STRICTLY IN ADVANCE

If you have not seen the *Journal*, write for a specimen copy. There is nothing like it. The name of every banjo and guitar player should be found upon our subscription list, which is constantly increasing.

Those sending 50 cents for subscription to the *Journal* may name any one of the following premiums, which will be mailed free. Each subscriber is entitled to **one** premium only.

## ········ PREMIUM LIST ········

"The Guitarist's Delight"—A book of selections for guitar, value . . . . . . . . . $ .25

"The Banjo and Guitar Music Album"—A book of music; some for the banjo and some for guitar . . value .25

Book, "The Banjo"—Bound in paper cover . . " .25

"Banjo and Guitar Budget"—Another good collection of music; partly for banjo and partly for guitar value .25

"Portfolio of Banjo Music"—A nice collection of banjo pieces . . . . . . . . value .25

"The Banjoist's Assistant"—Chart of the banjo fingerboard . . . . . . . . value .25

Any one of these premiums is well worth the price of subscription, and the *Journal* is a host in itself.

# Standard Books of Instruction
## FOR BANJO STUDENTS

Published by S. S. STEWART, Philadelphia, Pa.

**The Complete American Banjo School,** by S. S. Stewart.

Part First, . . . . . . . . . . , $1.00; postage, 13c. extra
Part Second, . . . . . . . . . . 1.00; " 8c. "
Complete, both parts, in board cover, 2.00; " 26c. "

The above work is believed to be the most thorough and complete work on the banjo extant. The price has been reduced to the above figure in order that the work may be easily within reach of all. Those who wish the instruction and explanatory matter alone, without the musical selections, need purchase *part first* only, as that volume contains all of the rudimentary and explanatory matter, exercises, chords, scales, etc., while *part second* contains musical selections.

**Rudimental Lessons for the Banjo,** by S. S. Stewart. Parts 1 and 2; each part, 25c., postage free.

Chart of the Banjo Fingerboard, full size

**The Banjoist's Assistant** or Note Reading made easy. 25c.

Postage free. This chart is very useful to beginners, showing all the notes of the staff, connected with the frets on the fingerboard of the banjo.

**Stewart's Thorough School for the Banjo,** price, $1.00

This is an older and not as complete work as the "American School" of the same writer, but is a good work. The price has been reduced to the above figure. It was formerly sold for $2.00 per copy.

**The Young Banjoist,** by S. S. Stewart . . . . price, $1.00

A very good book of quite easy selections for young players and containing some rudimentary instruction.

**The Artistic Banjoist,** . . . . . . . . . . price, $1.00

A collection of choice music for the banjo, edited by S. S. Stewart. This collection should be in the hands of every banjo player.

**The Banjoist's Own Collection of Choice**
**Music,** . . . . . . . . . . . . . . . . price, 50c.

This is a very excellent collection of banjo music, well arranged, and it is doubtful if it can be duplicated for the small price.

# THE WORKS OF JOHN H. LEE

.....FOR THE BANJO.....

PUBLISHED BY S. S. STEWART, PHILADELPHIA, PA.

## Eclectic School for the Banjo,

Published in three parts, the prices of which have been reduced to the following:

| | |
|---|---|
| **Part First,** Instruction, | $ .75 |
| **Part Second,** Musical Selections | 1.50 |
| **Part Third,** Chord Construction, | .50 |

Part First is an excellent rudimentary work and is very successful in teaching pupils to read music at sight.

Part Second contains some of the author's choicest arrangements of instrumental music for the banjo, and those who are familiar with Mr. Lee's work recognize his arrangements as among the most correct and thorough ever given to banjo players.

Every banjo student should have these valuable works in his library.

## National School for the Banjo, by Alfred A. Farland

### Price, . . . . . . . $1.00

Those hearing Mr. Farland render his marvelous banjo music will no doubt be glad to come in contact with his excellent instruction book, the "National School for the Banjo." This work teaches his original methods of fingering, and contains some twenty fine concert solos, together with exercises and scales in all keys.

No enlightened banjoist of this epoch can afford to be contented with only one method—he should make himself familiar with all. We heartily commend this work to all students of the banjo. Copies mailed on receipt of price.

## "Banjo Orchestra Music;" Hints to Arrangers
### and Leaders of Banjo Clubs, by Thomas J. Armstrong, . . . . . . . . . . . . . Price, 50 Cents

This is an invaluable book to those interested in banjo, mandolin and guitar clubs. Copies mailed on receipt of price.

# The Banjo Philosophically

**Its** Construction, **Its** Capabilities, **Its**
Evolution, **Its place as a Musical**
**Instrument.** Its possibilities,
**and** Its future.

## A LECTURE
By S. S. STEWART.

I have selected as my subject THE PHILOSOPHICAL PRINCIPLES OF THE BANJO AND BANJO PLAYING. More properly speaking, I should say, THE PHILOSOPHICAL BASIS ON WHICH THE BANJO IS CONSTRUCTED, AND THE PHILOSOPHY OF BANJO PLAYING.

I have here several banjos and parts which it is my purpose to introduce, and which I shall use as objects of illustration during the course of my lecture.

I ask your attention, for a short time, to my remarks, and I will endeavor to bring before you, in as unpretentious manner as possible, the different classes and grades of banjos, and notice briefly the various changes which have taken place in the instrument during the past thirty years, during its process of evolution to its present state of progression.

The banjo is, as you all know, an instrument of the stringed class, and may be associated with the guitar, lute, mandolin, bandore, etc. I believe, and it is so stated by other authorities, that the banjo got its name from the bandore, and that it is not of negro origin as has been claimed.

The bandore some of you have heard played, when you listened to the Original Spanish Students,

It is of ancient origin and the name banjo is thought to have been corrupted therefrom.

There is no such instrument as a bandoline, so far as my knowledge extends, although I have heard that name mentioned in connection with banjos.

Bandoline, as I understand it, is a hair oil or pomade, and can have no signification here,

The name **Banjeaurine** has been given to a somewhat modern style of banjo of my own manufacture, and of which I shall have something to say presently.

I mentioned some time ago in a small publication relating to the banjo, that an Egyptian Lyre of the Ancient Egyptians had been seen by a certain writer, which was in every respect a modern banjo. I believe that the hoop or rim of this lyre was oblong or oval, and not circular, like ours—hence it was not a "modern banjo."

However, it is not my purpose to delve into by-gone ages, searching after fragments of the past—at least not at this time; nor is it my purpose to dwell upon the origin and ancestry of the present banjo, nor to occupy any more of your time by dwelling upon or discussing as to where, why, when and how the banjo got its name.

We all admit that it has a name and that its name is banjo b-a-n-j-o or b-a-n-j-e-a-u, but not ba-n-j-e-r. This is sufficient.

The instrument, as it stands, is composed of a circular frame or rim, over which a membraneous substance, called the head, is stretched. This head being elastic acts as a sound-board, as does also, in a manner, the wood or other material in the rim or circular frame.

The instrument, like the guitar and other instruments of its class, has a neck; from the extreme end of which strings are stretched, extending over the head, across the circular frame.

A small piece of wood is fashioned into a "bridge," upon which the strings rest, and by which their vibration is conducted to the head. Without this small appendage, the bridge, the instrument would be worthless.

The banjo differs in the tone produced, as well as in its shape and general appearance, from the guitar and other instruments of the same class.

The strings vibrate, and are treated in a similar manner to the strings upon a guitar, but the philosophy and scientific principles of the construction of the instrument are different.

In the banjo the head combines its vibration or pulsations with the vibrations of the strings, and the rim acts in unison with the head as a peculiar kind of sound-board. But of this I shall have more to say later on.

## THE EARLY BANJO.

Should any of you open *Moore's Encyclopedia of Music* at page 90, and there read its description of a banjo, you would possibly be led to believe that the banjo was not much of a musical instrument. And you would infer rightly; for at the time the *Encyclopedia* was published, in the year 1854, I believe, the banjo was considered, as some have it, purely an instrument of accompaniment. In those days no one supposed that the banjo would ever become a recognized and favorite musical instrument, or that it could ever possibly become a favorite with the ladies.

Time works great changes, and yet I have no doubt that many there are who still have no other conception of the banjo than as described in Moore's and other Encyclopedias.

About the first player upon the banjo I have heard spoken of was Joe Sweeney, of Virginia. Before his day the instrument is said to have been a "three-string gourd," and played by one Picayune Butler, of whom many of you have heard. There was a great old-time "banjo song," said to have been sung by him, called *"Picayune Butler's Come to Town."*

But as Picayune Butler's Three String Gourd bears as little relation to the present banjo as the ancient *Viol* does, or did, to our present *Violin,* the king of musical instruments, I deem it worthy of but brief mention at present.

148

Sweeney, aforesaid, is said to have added the third and filth strings to the "three string gourd" and made it, what was at that time called a banjo.

The banjo at that time had no hoop and system of screw hooks to tighten the head. The head or skin was usually fastened to the rim with tacks and cement.

The head, after being wet, was stretched over the circular rim, which was usually of ash wood, and then fastened and allowed to dry.

When the head dried it of course contracted and became firm and tight. We have still in use almost the identical system for putting heads on tambourines, but the old-fashioned "tack head" banjo has gone out of date—burned out, like a taper or tallow dip, which has given place to the lamp, gas jet and electric light.

Following the "tack head" banjo came the screw- head banjo with solid iron hand or hoop and iron brackets and screws.

It was no longer necessary to hold the banjo near a stove in order to cause the head to contract and become tight when the weather was damp, as the nuts upon the hooks could ht screwed up and the hoop drawn down in a somewhat similar manner as it is done today.

But the banjo at best was a very crude instrument. The system, or mechanical part of the same, was very unfinished, and the heads in use were generally made of sheepskin, and were not calculated to stand the strain which those used to-day are put to.

The necks, too, were very crude, and generally had a piece of wood sliced out of the butt-end, adjoining the rim and hoop, as nobody ever thought of playing "Away up There" in those days.

Then, too, the instrument was strung with thick strings and tuned to a low pitch, and the style of execution was entirely the old "stroke," or original "banjo style." Nobody "picked" the banjo then in what is now termed "guitar style"

They used to make the banjo rims in those days at least three inches in depth, which made them look clumsy and "tubby."
In those days there was a banjo maker in New York by the name of Jacobs. He is spoken of as the first "professional banjo maker," or first maker of "professional banjos." That means that he did not make fancy banjos for the ladies to decorate with ribbons and hang up in their boudoirs, but he made a good, solid, strong, heavy-built banjo, which was calculated to stand the hard knocks of the minstrel stage.

I have never, so far as I know, seen or played upon one of Jacobs' instruments, but I think if I could produce one of them that you would scarcely recognize in it any resemblance to our favorite "silver-rim" banjo of to-day, now so popular.

Jacobs was evidently an industrious German, and returned to his native land with a small fortune, made by hard work and saved by frugal living.

It may be that he introduced into Germany the patterns from which some factories are still turning out banjos, but I hesitate to charge an honest man with such a crime. However, Jacobs lived and made his banjos before my time, that is, before I saw the light in this world; and I will refrain, therefore, from raking over the ashes of by-gone days, now buried in oblivion.

From time to time improvements were made in the banjo as it developed in the hands of new performers. Mechanics here and there improved its various parts, and gradually musicians "took hold" of it.

More brackets were added to the rim; some makers narrowed down their rims a little, and also shortened their necks, and then banjos began to appear having polished brass or German silver brackets and hooks instead of iron. A gaudy brass plate was sometimes set into the neck as a part of the finger-board.

Players began to execute music in the guitar style of playing, and the instrument became a great attraction in all minstrel shows.

G. Swayne Buckley was one of the first who added the guitar style of *frets* to his banjo, although I believe that he played almost entirely "banjo" or "stroke" style, and therefore his wisdom in using *frets* (raised frets) was doubted by many.

At that time scarcely any performer used frets, raised or otherwise—on a banjo neck. Indeed there would have been little use for them with most of the "great banjo soloists" of that day, as they never thought of stopping the strings beyond the fifth string peg. The gigantic effort required in making a *barre cbord* on the banjo then used was not to be indulged in by any, save those of advanced musical views and good physical development.

I have endeavored to be as brief as possible in my remarks, as the ground already covered is but an introduction to what follows. I will, therefore, now take up the THE BANJO—. *the silver rim banjo*—which I consider the only true banjo, and endeavor to philosophise and analyze the instrument in as few words as possible.

# THE "SILVER RIM" BANJO.

Just as there are enormous numbers of trade fiddles, cheap violins, turned out of the great toy shop of the world, Germany, and sold by our music stores throughout the land, so there are factories in this country, where large numbers of cheap banjos are manufactured and supplied to the trade.

The old style "tack-head" banjo *is* scarcely found in a music store to-day, but it is sometimes to be found at toy stores, where they are disposed of to young ladies, some of whom purchase them for cheap decorating purposes. But the majority of banjos turned out by the "cheap factories" at this time are metal covered rim banjos, with nickel plated mountings and walnut necks. They arc made in imitation of the Standard German Silver Rim "Professional" Banjo, and sold to beginners and learners of the instrument. Nearly all of my recent customers have had at least one of these cheap banjos. In fact I prefer that such should be the case, as a person who has been in the habit of playing upon a poor instrument is all the more ready to appreciate a good one when he gets it, although it may be that his "musical ear" has become deadened to some extent.

Many of you have heard of the old" Troy Banjo." A few years ago these banjos were in use by many players upon the stage and thought much of. They were made by two makers: The first was Albert Wilson, an eccentric genius, who was much liked by many players of his day. Wilson was followed by a maker named William H. Farnham, who followed the style originated by Wilson, without attempting any important improvement. These banjos were generally of 10 1/2, 11 and 11 1/2 inch rim. The necks were bolted fast to the rims, there being no wood or metal bar extending from the neck through the rim as there is in nearly all banjos of the present day. The absence of this bar caused the neck to constantly work upwards, and the banjo could not be depended upon to remain in tune.

The rims of these instruments were constructed upon the same principles as those of to-day. A maple wood hoop, covered with sheet German silver, and turned down at each side over a wire ring. But the work was more crude at that period, and the rims, although very strong and solidly made, were not capable of giving the vibration of those produced and used this day in the Stewart Banjo. This is a well attested fact.

The "Clarke Banjo," an improvement on the Wilson and Farnham Banjos, became a general favorite among minstrel and other stage performers.

Clarke's Banjos were made by the late Jas. W. Clarke, who continued to make them until the time of his death, which was caused by consumption, and took place in New York City, on February 27th, 1880. Clarke's Banjos, as I have said, were an improvement on the Wilson or Farnham instrument, as Clarke added the extension bar to the necks, making the instrument more solid in construction, and more sure to remain in tune. But I do not mean to say that Clarke was by any means the inventor of this improvement, or that it was of his own origination, for the majority of wood rim banjos, even before that day, were so made. But every manufacturer of a musical instrument leaves the impress of his individuality in his work, to a certain extent. This is a perfectly philosophical and a well known psychological fact, and governed by a psychological law.

Outside of this, Clarke had his little secrets in regard to his methods of work, just as every skilled workman and specialist has to-day, and as well, many little points which would scarcely be of much service to another maker, for every true genius has his natural and original ways of working.

Clark's banjos were noted for their loud and sharp tone, it being a standard among professional banjo players, that if you wanted a "sharp banjo" you must get a Clarke.     There are makers to-day, who, instead of branching out and studying their subject, and endeavoring to get up instruments better than others, which is the only legitimate way in which a demand for their instruments can be created are content to plod along, copying the *Clarke Banjo* and the patterns of other makers.

Such makers very seldom amount to anything. No two men have the same individuality, and hence it is basis of construction, in fad is constructed in as folly for one man to copy another. The true banjo maker needs no copy, his model is formed in the mind, and he works out his own ideas. Those makers who possess no ideas of their own had better, far better, try some other means of gaining a livelihood.

On the other hand, we have manufacturers who are constantly inflicting upon the banjo what they are pleased to designate as "improvements," some of which are patented.

We have had patent-closed backs, patent hoops, of brackets, which are so made as to admit of hooks patent hollow rims, patent bell rims, patent keys, with screw threads cut on them passing through them, patent bracket protectors, patent tail pieces, patent and a variety of other patents; but none of these have added one jot nor tittle to the musical value of the banjo.

The "silver-rim banjo," as described, has been for years past the standard banjo; THE BANJO among professional players of note, and the number of "patent banjos" of any kind in use by noted players, or even skilled amateurs, has always been very small.

There are, and have been, "wooden-rim" banjos in use on the stage at various times by performers, and although the great majority of this class of banjos may be rated as "tubs," yet a really good instrument of wood rim is sometimes to be found.

And yet, in these banjos, there is almost always to be found metal of some kind, combined with the wood. It may be only an iron or brass strip or wire ring, intended merely to strengthen the rim, but it nevertheless has its effect upon the tone of the instrument.

I can, therefore, confidently assert that the standard banjo, with players of eminence and skill, is a banjo with a metal and wood rim used in combination.

The Stewart Banjos, as manufactured by myself at the present time, are simply claimed to be improvements upon the same style of banjo manufactured by others before me.

On my banjos proper I claim no new invention, nor have I any patents connected therewith. (This remark has no reference to the improved *Banjeaurine*)

But I do claim an improved and more perfected banjo, secured by new processes of manufacture, some of which remain secrets of my own, and which to attempt to protect by letters patent would merely place part of my knowledge in the hands of others. I also claim a skill in the construction of banjos, the result of a *natural musical gift,* together with a somewhat extended experience as a performer upon the instrument, and a student of the science of music, which, together with experimenting and constant observation, has aided me, and added to my adaptability in this, my particular line of business.

Without any egotistical feelings whatever, I am able to point with pride to the letters from our most talented, prominent and eminent players of the banjo; in fact, foremost artists of the day, testifying to the merits of the banjos manufactured by me, and of their many points of superiority over the instruments of other manufacturers.

I do not assert that the banjos I manufacture are perfect; nor do I believe that those of any other maker are perfect; or that anything produced on this earth is or ever has been *perfect*. But whatever assertions regarding my banjos I have made have been certified to and fully indorsed; in fact, more fully than I have ever asked, by players of eminence who have no pecuniary interest whatever in my business or my banjos.

Neither do I assume to know all there is to be learned about banjo making or any other art, science or philosophy. What I may know to-day I may discover, tomorrow, that I do not know. What seems in place to-day may seem out of place to-morrow, and vice versa.

I expect to learn something new every day, and all that can be expected of me to-day is that I shall give you my views and ideas as they exist at the present time.

I have asserted, and can readily demonstrate by letters from leading players, that the banjo of *German silver and wood combined rim* is and has been for a long time *the banjo*—the recognized banjo of the artist banjo player.

This banjo has a perfectly scientific and philosophical basis of construction, in fact is constructed in as philosophically correct a manner as the guitar, mandoline, zither or any other stringed instrument. Its body consists of a circular frame, called the rim. This rim, as you will notice, has a bright and attractive appearance. It is composed of the alloy known as German silver on the outside, and maple wood upon the inside. They are, in fact, two separate and distinct rims so united as to act as one.

We attach to this combination, or rim, a system of brackets, which are so made as to admit of hooks with screw threads cut on them passing through them, and a suitable nut being fitted to each of the several screws.

With these hooks or screws, and by the aid of this bright and neatly-finished band or hoop, we are enabled to adjust the important factor called the head. The head is a membrane or membraneous skin, and is, as shown, adjusted and tightly stretched upon or over the rim or circular frame.

When this is completed we have, as you see before you, the body of the instrument almost complete.

Next, we have the neck of walnut, maple, cherry, rose or other suitable wood, which must be accurately fitted and correctly adjusted to the body of the instrument. We call the upper surface of the neck the *finger-board,* for over this surface the strings are stretched, which are vibrated to produce the musical sounds. Were it not for this neck surface, the finger-board, we should have only five notes or sounds, as produced by the five strings of the banjo.

This is, of course, speaking only for the regular five-string banjo; some banjos being constructed with additional strings. The musical strings are stretched from the appendage called the *tail-piece,* which, by the way, was often termed *apron* in days gone by; so termed, I presume, from its large size and close resemblance to the article of female dress designated by that name—over the extreme end of the finger-board, running through notches in this little piece of ivory called the nut, to the pegs, by the turning of which we are enabled to tighten the strings or alter their tension, either one way or the other at pleasure. The bridge—this insignificant little piece of maple— over which the strings pass, rests firmly upon the head in the position you see in this instrument.

Without the bridge the banjo would be useless as a musical instrument.

When the strings are set in vibration, which is done with the fingers of the right hand, the vibrations produce motion In the air, which we term *sound waves*. The sound waves being in close proximity to the head are reverberated by it, and the bridge acting as a conductor of sound, also transmits the vibrations to the head, which is elastic, and these double vibrations, so to speak, are transmitted through the air.

Thus the head acts as a sound-board by which the sound waves caused by the vibration of stretched strings are transmitted, and at the same time is itself a sonorous body, having, so to speak, an independent vibration, and thus plays a double part in the construction of the instrument.

The *rim,* too, plays an all-important part in the vibrating power of the instrument, and is, in fact, the entire foundation upon which the musical quality, quantity and power of the banjo's tone must be built.

The head, as I have shown, is tightly stretched over the rim, and is itself sonorous, the requisite necessary for producing sound of any kind.

The head having a flat, smooth surface, becomes an excellent sound-board, and being circular in shape, is well calculated to transmit sound waves, which are, so to speak, floating circles.

The head thus tightly drawn over the rim acts in unison therewith. It must act in unison with the rim or we will have a poor banjo.

Thus the head and the rim are united, they are parts of one whole; they must unite and become as ONE just as surely as the pine-wood top of the guitar becomes one with the guitar when it is attached thereto by glue.

The vibration of the strings then, it is conceded, is conducted to the head by means of the bridge, and to the rim by means of the head, and the rim must he so constructed as **to** respond to and mingle its vibrations with those of the head and strings, forming one harmonious whole.

When the head is wet or damp it is slack, and when in that condition the banjo will not produce a very good tone.

The reason for this is because the sounding quality, or sonorousness of any substance depends upon its hardness and elasticity, and when the head is wet or damp it lacks the necessary hardness, and has not the required elasticity.

Another reason is that when the head is loose and flabby there is not sufficient tension upon the rim to cause it to properly respond to the vibrations of the head, which are much slower than when the head is drawn tight.

What is called a "sharp" tone in the banjo is regulated, 1st. By the tension of the strings, which in all cases regulate its musical pitch.

2d. By the quality, size, tension, elasticity and hardness of the head.

3d. By the size, weight and sonorous qualities of the rim and length of neck. In fact, I might say that these different points regulate and govern the quality of its tone entirely, be it sharp or fiat, musical or Un- musical, harmonious or discordant.

The strings which when picked or struck just as they stand, produce each *one* separate tone, but as upon the guitar or violin, we can, by making use of the fingerboard, "stop" the strings so as to produce all the notes of the chromatic scale, from C below the staff to C alt.

This is done by placing a given finger of the left hand upon the string, and holding it firmly to the finger-board at the proper position, thus allowing only a portion of the string, instead of the entire string to vibrate. Thus, by making all the stops at the proper positions upon the finger-board, we can cause the strings to produce all the various notes just as readily as though each were produced by a separate string.

Or, we can construct the finger-board with *raised frets,* similar to the guitar, and, as you see in the banjo I introduce, by stopping the string *between* the frets the string is brought down on the fret, and of course vibrates only between the fret at which it is stopped and the bridge, in place of the entire string vibrating as would he the case if the string was allowed to vibrate without being stopped. (Vibrate its whole length.) It is well here to say a few words in regard to the difference between the tone produced by the banjo and that produced by the guitar, its sister in a musical sense.

**RELATIVELY.**

The timbre of the banjo's tone is brilliant and enlivening, whilst that of the guitar is more subdued, soft and soothing. When the strings of the guitar are caused to vibrate, their agitation compresses the air body within the instrument, and this air body instantly expands, and aided by the back of the guitar proceeds forth in sound waves.

The top of the guitar is generally constructed of pine or deal, whilst the back is composed of maple or rosewood, as are also the sides. It has a sound bole in the top, circular in shape, from which its vibrations proceed.

The character, quality or power of tone in this instrument depends:

1st. Upon its model or size.

2d. Upon the quality and tension of the strings and the bridge upon which they rest

3d. Upon the thickness of its top and back.

4th. Upon the sonorous and general acoustical properties of the woods used.

5th. Upon the quantity and specific density of the air body between the back and top (or within the instrument.)

6th. Upon the perfect fitting and adjustment of, and the harmonious action and relation of all its parts, inclusive of blocks and braces within the instrument.

The guitar is best adapted for music of a pensive and soothing character, and at the present day is not in use to any extent as a concert instrument.

Generally, the full power of tone a guitar is capable of producing may be had, by a player in good practice, by picking the strings with the fingers, and any attempt at striking the strings downward with a view to produce a greater quantity or volume of tone, only causes the instrument to give a less melodious and somewhat confused tone.

The guitar is plainly not suited to nor adapted for powerful or "noisy" music. It is a beautiful instrument when played by the hands of a master, whose mind is in harmony with its sphere of action.

### "STROKE BANJOS"

In a banjo we sometimes find the tones produced by ticking the strings to be acute and brilliant, and yet lacking the power or intensity' necessary for a solo instrument; and yet in the same instrument, by striking the strings with a light metal thimble constructed for that purpose, the power and volume of tone be. comes augmented to a wonderful extent.

Such banjos are frequently called "stroke" or "thimble" banjos, because they are better adapted for stroke playing or thimble execution than for picking, or playing guitar style.

It is conceded that the strings being vigorously struck, and the vibration being conducted, by means of the bridge, to the head, that the head is caused to vibrate more intensely and vigorously than when the strings are only "picked." Then these vibrations are in a like vigorous manner communicated to the rim, its sounding-frame, which being agitated, mingles with or contributes to the sound.

This is a philosophical fact, provided the banjo is correctly constructed.

## THE NECESSARY CONSTITUENTS.

What then are the requisites in a good-toned, or fine-sounding banjo?

1st. An acuteness of sound or tone.

2d. Musical purity of tones and free vibration.

3d. Intensity of tone, resonance, carrying power.

4th. Easy action and equalization of upper and lower register.

In toto: The banjo must have a *musical tone,* and at the same time, not relinquish its "banjo" characteristics or individuality, and there must also be sufficient *resonance* of sound.

What then is necessary in the construction of a good banjo; and how must a banjo be constructed so as to meet the requirements of an artist? I think I hear some one say," It must be made perfect, or as nearly so as possible, in all its parts and -the pails must all be fitted correctly."

This is very good, and true so far as it goes. I hear another answer, "It must have a good head on."

Excellent! true again, but why not add, "a good set of strings," for we could make no music without them.

Let me ask you, where can you find am instrument, tool, engine or a machine of any kind whatsoever, which is satisfactory in any way or capable of doing good work unless it is properly constructed, adjusted and correctly fitted in all its parts?

And yet, it is possible to construct a **machine** which is correctly made, adjusted and properly fitted in all its parts, and yet produce a machine which is incapable of doing the work it is intended for. The model may have been all wrong. The inventor may have in his mind, when he conceived his idea, been wrong or mistaken in his calculations as to the compass and capability of his machine.

In this case a perfect making of the various parts together with correct fitting of the same, has not produced the result aimed at, simply because the entire foundation of the work was wrong. Just so it may be with a banjo.

What then is necessary?

1st. The head should be of even thickness, neither too thin nor too thick.

2d. The strings must be of the right kind and quality.

3d. The wood in the inner rim must be selected with a view to sonorousness or acoustical qualities. It should be properly seasoned and correctly treated and shaped.

4th. The German silver or other sheet metal for outer rim should be of the right temper, uniform thickness and density, and properly rolled. It must also be perfectly and evenly brazed.

5th. The neck should be of wood selected with a view to lightness, strength, sonorousness and non liability to warp or change with atmospheric changes.

6th. The "wire edge" must be so constructed as to act as a ready conductor of sound, and at the same time resist the strain of the head upon the rim. This "wire edge" ring must be of the right thickness, proper specific density, uniform in thickness, and composed of a suitable metal. It must also be accurately adjusted in making the rim.

7th. The wood rim, sheet metal rim and wire edges must all be constructed upon acoustical and scientific principles, and must likewise be united as a whole upon a philosophical basis.

8th. The neck must be properly fitted to the rim and adjusted to suit the tension of the strings.

9th. The neck should be so veneered as to withstand climatic changes as much as possible, and to resist the strain of constant changes in pitch of the strings.

10th. The wire ring called "flesh hoop," around which the head is wrapped, should be so constructed as to securely hold the head from slipping, and the band or hoop whose place it is to draw the head tight and secure it in position, should be so constructed as to hold the head evenly all around the circle, and not permit the ends of the hooks to press against or cut the head.

11th. The bridge must be of the right height, width and thickness, and constructed of wood having the necessary acoustical properties.

12th. If the banjo finger-board is fretted, the frets must be so gauged that the bridge has its proper position upon the head.

All the parts of the instrument must, of course, be harmoniously blended and correctly joined and fitted.

All of these points, merely outlined here, should be studied by the true banjo maker. And there still remain many others to be considered, such as varnishing, polishing, gluing, etc, etc. The weight and number of brackets is also a very important point.

In the making of cheap grade banjos, such as are now largely found in music shops and pawnbrokers' establishments, very few of these points need be considered, if indeed, any of them are considered at all by wholesale manufacturers.

But as cheap grade banjos, like "trade fiddles," are not intended for *artists,* it is of little signification to us how they are constructed, and I will therefore pass but a few remarks concerning their manufacture.

## "Trade Banjos" and "Store Tubs."

It sounds rather homely to designate a gaudy banjo having a cart load of brackets (more or less), a "Store Tub," and yet they are often designated by such an appellation. Nick-names are wont to stick when they once take hold. The time is coming when a large number of brackets upon a banjo will cause it to be looked upon with suspicion. At the present time the commonest banjos made are covered with brackets in order to catch the eye of the passer by.

One has only to walk a short distance to come across a store window where this class of banjo is displayed.

In the factories where these instruments are manufactured the work is done almost entirely by steam- power machinery, whilst in the higher grade of banjos only a portion of the work can be done in this way.

Cheap necks are made in large quantities, by special machines, in a manner somewhat similar to which gun-stocks and ax-handles are turned out.

They are veneered, if veneered at all, with a single strip, as no machine has been devised for gluing on veneers. These necks are sand-papered on "buffs," run also upon steam lathes.

The wooden rims are glued up to as uniform a size as possible, after which they are "turned up" on lathes and sand-papered at the same time.

This work, to insure cheapness, must he done in large quantities, or a large number manufactured at one time.

The metal part of the rim in cheap banjos is generally made of sheet brass, nickel-plated.

The sheet metal is cut to a gauge in strips of uniform size, brazed together, formed up, spun and nickel plated; after which the already-made wooden rim is fitted into it.

If the cheap rim is to be "wired" on both edges, one edge is generally left until after the wood is in.

The wire edges in these banjos are placed there in order to give the instrument a finish, and to strengthen the rim.

The cheap necks are generally set in tire rims, that is, the holes cut in the rims either with a cold chisel or punch made for the purpose, by boys; anything to facilitate the work.

The holes for brackets are bored with a drill, the lathe of which runs by steam, and the brackets and heads are put on and the hoops fitted, mostly by boys.

Different shops and different mechanics employ various methods. I am only generalizing here.

The banjos are strung up and sold, and I doubt if the majority of them are tested or tried, or if bridges are ever fitted to them before they leave the factories.

Cheap banjos are largely sold to the stores through wholesale jobbing houses, who import and whole sale musical goods, and have drummers or selling agents constantly on the road with samples.

They are sold, generally, by the dozen, at so much per dozen, half dozen, or quarter dozen, and regardless of age, sex, color or previous condition.

You may get a good one- you may get a poor one. The purchaser must take his chances as to that. Nearly every learner of the banjo has to make his experience, and must needs buy one or more "store tubs" before he is fully prepared to purchase a good instrument. The same rule applies to beginners with all other instruments. It is the same with the guitar, with the violin, with the zither, with the flute, with band instruments, and in fact with all musical instruments.

If this were not the case good instruments would not be appreciated. Wholesale manufacturers of cheap instruments cater to the eye first—the ear afterwards.

They know that nearly all beginners will buy a cheap instrument to learn on, and that a large proportion of those who buy cheap banjos or other instruments will never make anything but mediocre players, and will not know the difference between a good or poor instrument, so long as they have the same appearance in outer respects.

Then, too, the prices of cheap instruments suit the pockets of the majority better than expensive instruments.

These facts account for the enormous number of cheap banjos manufactured and sold in this country, as well as for the large number of cheap guitars imported and placed upon the American market.

But in the manufacture of a high grade banjo the work cannot be greatly cheapened by the employment of steam-power machinery; nor can it in the manufacture of a high grade guitar or violin.

In the higher priced banjos there is a certain amount of testing to be done at each step of the way, and the banjos cannot be made up in quantities with success: Each instrument requires separate consideration. Steam-power machinery can be utilized in the rough work, such as band sawing, shaping out, etc.; also in metal spinning, turning, etc. But much of the work must be done by hand, nevertheless.

The necks in fine banjos are sawed out, shaped, veneered, etc., many months before they find their way into the instrument they are intended for. Were not this the case we should be troubled continually by necks warping, and even with long seasoning of wood, etc., we often find that a neck will warp after it is ready for finishing.

Sometimes the addition of a single veneer will cause a neck to warp, and it has taken me a long time, and cost considerable money to arrive at the proper methods of making and treating necks. I have not the time to speak upon this part of the subject at length, but merely to touch upon it briefly. The subject of banjo necks alone would require a complete lecture were I to attempt to dwell upon it to any length.

As I have already stated, there are many points of detail in connection with banjo making which I am not prepared to touch upon at all, for the present, they being held as secrets of my business. And even were I disposed to enter into details it would require a book of at least 500 pages to cover the ground, and moreover, I am continually making new discoveries and consequently improvements.

Sufficient to say that very frequently after a banjo is entirely finished it must needs be taken apart and the work "done over again.". This is the case when plenty of time is allowed for the making of a fine instrument, and when upon its being finished I have not found the tone entirely satisfactory.

It is sometimes the case that a well made and properly constructed banjo may sound poorly by reason of its having upon it a poor head, or a head not adapted to the instrument. In this case, when the head is removed and replaced by one which is the proper thing, the banjo will be found greatly improved in tone.

But if the banjo has upon it a good, even head, properly stretched, and does not sound well, there is small chance for improvement by changing, heads. Not more than one change is recommended in any such instance.

You may have heard it said that any poor sounding banjo could be made to sound well by changing the head, but I tell you that an improperly constructed banjo cannot be made into a good instrument by changing the head. Experience has taught me that this is a fact. My musical knowledge and the study of acoustics also teaches me that any such idea' is an utter fallacy.

Banjo making, in fact all musical instrument king, like the science of music so called, is a science only to a certain extent. It is an art, an art based upon scientific principles.

A man Cannot make a good musician, never mind how much science he may have in him, unless he is *artist*. The same rule applies to musical instrument making.

I have heard it said that a violin could be improved breaking *it* up and glueing it together again. I have heard it said that a banjo could be improved by baking the rim in an oven. I have heard a great my other funny things and so have you. I don't believe all I hear, neither do you. Perhaps if you should take a good guitar or violin to some excellent mechanic (worker in woods), who had no acquaintance with music or musical instruments, and ask him he could make you a duplicate of either instrument, he might answer "yes."

He would probably reason that all he had to do would be to follow the original as a model, gauge and measure, using precisely the same kinds of wood and varnish, and having produced an exact copy of the original the tone must necessarily be the same. But you all know that the chances are ninety nine out of a hundred that his copy would not sound anything like his model.

Why is it?

Why do not copies of the famous Cremona violins sound equally as well as the Cremonas?

"Perhaps they do," you answer.

Well, thousands of eminent artists in violin playing assert that they *do not,* and very few assert that they *do.* So why is it ?

Science has never been able to demonstrate clearly to why it is.

Some say that it is *age* alone which gives the Cremona violin its superior tone. Some say that it is owing to the peculiar qualities of the woods then used. Others say it is *owing* to the long use of the instruments.

Some seem to think that it is the rosin dust, which in the course of time has an action on the wood. And we have many fine spun theories—some of them exceedingly fallacious and supremely ridiculous.

Volumes have been written and published upon this subject, and many there are who consider violin making lost art.

I believe that the ancient Italian masters worked upon perfectly scientific principles. They concentrated the entire powers of their minds upon their work, and worked slowly and with harmonious surroundings. They understood the different specific qualities of their maple and pine woods. The climate of their country was adapted to the growth and seasoning of the woods used. I also believe that they care guided in their work by the same inspiration which guided the Italian painters of the same age. The Cremona masters were *true men* they followed their minds' ideal and did not copy the forms designed others.

Such of these old violins as have had the good fortune to escape the hands of some of our modern repairers I believe are good yet, but there are few of them in existence.

I do not believe that age alone ever made a good violin out of a poor one, but I believe that age, together with proper care and the use of the instrument a good musician, will improve, rather than injure good violin.

I do not believe that age can act upon the wood, after it has been once thoroughly seasoned (as all the woods used in these violins were) in a manner to cause the tone to improve. But I believe that vibration exerts a powerful influence upon wood and other substances. The full powers, uses and abuses of vibratory motion have not yet become known.

An instrument may become greatly improved in tone when played upon for a long time by a skillful performer, and the same instrument may become greatly impaired in tone by the discordant and unharmonious raspings of a musical botch.

The chief beauty in the old violins lies in their beautiful sweet tone and its carrying power. Not that the tone is loud, but that it can be heard a good distance, and is free from discordant elements.

A loud instrument is sometimes found to lack this power, and cannot be heard so far away as the softer toned instrument.

The philosophy of this is that pure sound will carry further than sound mixed with noise or discordant elements.

## EXPERIMENTS.

There have been some very interesting experiments made with old violins, as perhaps some of you have read.

Fetis, a distinguished writer upon the violin, says that a piece of figured maple wood of certain dimensions taken from the back of a violin made by Stradivarius, in the year 1757, produced the note A sharp, and another piece of plain maple from another instrument of the same maker, made in 1708—nine years previously—produced the same note.

He also says that a piece of deal or pine taken from he top of a violin of Stradivarius, made in the year 1724, produced the note F, and that another rod of deal from an instrument of the same master, made in 1690, gave also F, the same as from the violin made in 1724; and a third rod of deal obtained from anther instrument of this celebrated maker, made in 1730, also gave the same note, F.

I have in my possession a very fine copy of a Stradivarius violin, a copy of the year 1717 but the scope of this lecture will not permit me to dwell further upon the subject of violins, the few words I have said being merely illustrations of other remarks I hall make concerning banjos.

## SONOROUSNESS.

All woods, being to a greater or less degree hard and elastic, have the requisites for producing sound.

All *woods* yield some sound; all *metals* do not.

The specific sonorousness of wood was known to the ancient violin makers, it is known to day.

Maple and pine woods were used by the Cremona masters in their violins almost exclusively. The maple is often called *sycamore* in Europe, which has led students to suppose that the backs of violins were sometimes made of the wood of the Egyptian or Syrian fig tree. I prefer maple to-day, to any other wood for banjo rims. I have sometimes combined it with pine, but I consider the maple as indispensable. But this is saying almost nothing, for maple wood is of so many kinds and qualities that it takes time to study and learn how to distinguish its peculiar characteristics. It has been demonstrated by experiments made on various woods whose appearance was the same, that they yield diversities of sound. They vary greatly in pitch, sometimes a third, a fourth, or even more. Hence, should we select two pieces of wood, the same appearance, with which to make the backs of two violins, guitars or zithers, or the rims of two banjos, they (the woods) might possibly be widely different in pitch as well as in character of tone, Science cannot fully account for this, but experiment proves it to be a fact.

Coals of the same chemical composition, it is said, not always give out the same amount of heat. This fact has puzzled chemists for a long time.

Now if chemists are puzzled, and have been puzzled a long time as to why it is that coals of the same chemical composition give out various degrees of heat, it is fair to suppose that they might puzzle for a still longer period without finding out why it is that woods of the same appearance, size and weight, give various degrees of sound.

## WOODS.

Maple, Oak, Walnut, Cherry, Apple, Pear, Rose some other woods, each possess acoustical properties when properly selected and used in the right place.

---

176

All of these woods may be used in making banjo but in the long run I think maple gives the best satisfaction, although, of course, maple in itself may to a great degree in its sonorous qualities.

Two violins may be made from the same blocks of maple and pine, and yet be entirely unlike in musical qualities—one may be excellent and the other very poor. Such has been found to be the case frequently.

If we take a metal bar or rod and cut it in two, both pelts being the same, each part will sound the same note, which will be an octave higher in pitch than the whole bar sounded before it was cut in two. This is, of course, provided the bar is of equal thickness and weight throughout.

If we take a musical string and divide it in two by stopping it midway between its vibrating points, or on a banjo, between the nut and the bridge, half the string will sound the octave above the open or whole string. This is providing the string is of equal thickness throughout.

If we take two bars of wood, one bar half the length of the other, and each of the same thickness, the short bar will sound an octave above the long bar—but *not always*.

In a string, a very slight variance in thickness, so slight as scarcely to appear to the senses of touch or sight, and so slight as to escape the test of the string gauge, will cause it to sound "false," or not to vibrate in accordance with mathematical laws.

So it is with the bar of wood. A difference in the density or weight of two pieces of precisely the same size will often cause them to vary greatly in the pitch of sound produced, as well as in acoustical quality of tone. This is sometimes a difficulty encountered in the making of xylophones, and another well known fact is that a xylophone frequently goes out of tune after being made and tuned.

Chemical changes in the woods used, through processes of nature, changes of climate and other causes, operate to produce this. Hence it is that woods used in the construction of musical instruments must be thoroughly and prope4y seasoned, and philosophically treated in working.

To say that a piece of wood is extremely sonorous simply because it is maple, would be foolish, because all maple is not equally sonorous. There is an immense difference in it as there is in other woods. Take rosewood, for instance, a beautiful wood for veneering purposes. It comes from Brazil and other countries where the climate is warm, and is the product of several different kinds of trees. I might select a number of strips of this wood and each piece have an entirely different appearance, and yet it all goes by the same name.

Then take ebony, the wood used for finger-boards of banjos, violins, guitars, etc. It is so used because of its hardness and tendency to withstand wear, but it is a cracky wood, and must be treated and worked by those who understand it. It grows on the islands of Madagascar and Ceylon, and does not like our variable climate any better than some other close grained woods which grow in warm climates.

It is a mistaken idea with some of you that ebony is always black in color. Black is its usual color, but I have seen some that was red and other that was green. I have seen more which was black in some places, and of a light color in other places, Indeed, this is considered the best for finger-boards, not being so liable to crack. The light places may be stained so that the entire surface appears as black as may be desired. But I have not the time to go into minor details in this lecture, and I fear that I am wandering from the subject in hand.

German silver is an alloy composed of copper, nickel and zinc in various proportions, according to what it is intended to be used for. It may be hard or soft. If too hard it can be made softer by annealing. If too soft it may be made harder.

To say simply that German silver is a good metal for banjo rims is almost saying nothing at all, for so much depends upon its composition, its thickness, its temper, and the manner in which it is worked, as well as in the manner in which it is combined with other metals and woods used in the construction of an instrument.

It takes a fine polish, which is pleasing to the eye, and furthermore, may be nickel-plated, to as to retain its high finish for years.

German silver is sometimes called white copper, and sometimes called argentan, but I have always held to the name by which it is mostly known, although it might sound very nice to say that my banjo had an argentan rim or white copper hoop.

To say that a banjo has a bell-rim or a bell-metal rim, sounds nice to some persons, but the experienced performer wants whatever bell there may be in either the rim or in the metal to manifest itself through the medium of the strings when he plays upon the instrument.

If the banjo will not thus work it matters little whether the rim be composed of bell-metal, German silver, brass, copper, rosewood, maple or railroad iron.

The names of the various materials which enter into its

construction count for little if the instrument has not the tone desired by the performer.

BELL-M ETAL is an alloy of copper and tin. It is very hard, and consequently the metal workers do not like to work with it. Therefore if I should make a banjo rim of this metal it would have to be cast instead of being rolled and spun on lathes.

I do not consider it any better than brass or German silver to use in a banjo rim, if as good as either.

Now suppose I should take a bell—bells are supposed to be made of bell-metal—and suspend or fasten it within the banjo rim, or even hang it up anywhere near the banjo, so that the vibrations coming from the instrument would come in contact with the bell.

I now strike a chord upon the banjo, and then another, and so on. I keep on striking chords until I have struck the one which is in harmony with the bell.

Now the vibrations from the banjo have caused the bell to give forth a sound which mingles with the tone of the banjo.

You will perceive that the bell does not sound or add to the sound produced by the banjo excepting when this chord is struck—this chord which is in harmony with the bell.

If two strings are tuned perfectly to the same pitch, and one is set in vibration, the other will respond and add its vibration to the other. The one is in accord with the other—both producing, when vibrated, the same number of vibrations per second.

180

This will apply to all sounding bodies. The zither table for increasing the volume of sound from that instrument is constructed upon the same principle.

Now, if we desire to have the hell respond to each note made by the banjo, or to add to the tone produced by that instrument, it will be necessary to have a bell for each chord, as you will say, an impossibility.

Therefore, a bell in the rim of a banjo is like the fifth wheel to a coach—nearly always a useless encumbrance.

Such encumbrances are, in fact, not used by players who have made any degree of progress in the art of banjo playing.

Again, suppose I were to construct a rim of bell- metal or brass, something in the form of a bell, so that when suspended from a cord and struck, it would produce a bell-like tone, Do you imagine that this would add to the musical value or to the volume of sound produced by the banjo when its strings were struck?

It would do so only when the notes or chords, in unison or in harmony with the bell-shaped rim were used, whilst upon all the other notes or chords it would act as a damper and lessen the tone.

This is a philosophical fact and has been proven by experiment.

What kind of a bell (?) then, must the rim consist of in a good banjo, in order to produce a musical tone in all the notes and chords throughout the compass of the instrument?

1st. It must be a bell that is silent, except when you want it to speak.

2d. It must be a bell that, when it speaks, will sound equally well in all the tones of the instrument.

3d. It must be such a bell as will only ring when the strings are made to vibrate, and it must cause its presence to be known only through the medium of the vibrating strings, and never sound independent of them. In short, a *rim which is a dumb-bell—mute in itself, but sonorous when manifested through the strings of the banjo.* When you have learned to make such a rim you have acquired the first principles of making a good banjo.

The body of a Cremona violin is just such a bell as I have described, and yet the tone pitch of its top and back have been shown *not to have been tuned in unison.*

The musician knows that the chord of the *diminished seventh* when heard alone is discordant and disagreeable to the ear, but when used in its right place, and blended with or between concords, becomes harmonious and pleasing to the ear.

When I hear of banjo makers attempting to do away with all combinations of wood and metal in order to produce a musical tone, I Cannot help thinking of the fable of the fox, who, having lost his tail by reason of having been caught by it in a steel trap, in order to avoid the ridicule his appearance would create, hit upon the scheme of persuading all the foxes in his locality to cut off their tails and become like himself. It was impossible for this particular fox to retail himself, and so he wanted all the others to lose their tails also. Misery, it is said, loves company. "Grapes are sour to those who cannot get them."

Those who are not familiar with banjo making or its principles sometimes give vent to rather absurd ideas, and afflict the public with curious banjos. And those who cannot grasp an idea or evolve a principle sometimes seek to persuade themselves and customers that they are better off without what they cannot obtain.

Before I go any further I wish to say that I have no desire to "hit at" or criticize the methods pursued by other banjo manufacturers, nor to in anyway speak derogatory of their work or business. It is my desire, as far as conditions and circumstances will permit, to live in harmony with my fellow man, and when I mention forms of instruments manufactured by others in my line of business, I speak of them only in a general and illustrative manner, and mean nothing personal.

I have arrived at that point where I can look with pity upon a manufacturer, who, in his struggles to gain patronage, will resort to bogus challenges and "Champion of the World" methods and advertisements flaunting with unattested assertions. Vaunting his ignorance before a class of patrons even more ignorant than himself, and puffing himself as the patentee, inventor or claimant of inventions made before he had the misfortune to inflict the banjo fraternity with his presence.

I also look with pity upon the manufacturer who asserts and is psychologised by his ignorance into believing that he has made the banjo a perfect instrument, or has added more improvements to it than all others combined, and that all other manufacturers are his imitators.

On the other hand I am at all times ready to extend the hand of friendship to all sincere and honest makers or teachers of the banjo.

I am aware that various reports have been circulated concerning myself and methods of treating certain individuals, but the censure of some persons is almost, if not quite as valuable as the praise of others.

And again, if any of you were dealing with a skunk, you would not handle him in the same manner that you would use an animal of less odorous propensities. No, you would either get out of his way and let him alone, or else you would give him a dose of something more intensely clarifying than he was able to produce. But enough of this.

## MUSIC BY THE FOOT.

Many of you have heard the expression, used In connection with organs mostly,—" sixteen feet tone," "eight feet tone," etc., and probably few of you understand what is meant by such seemingly peculiar language.

An organ pipe eight feet long gives the great C, the lowest note and normal tone of the organ. A pipe half as long sounds the octave above, having double the number of vibrations per second. Whilst a pipe two feet in length vibrates four times as fast, and consequently sounds the next octave above, or two octaves higher than the first mentioned, and a pipe sixteen feet in length vibrates only half as fast as the pipe eight feet long and sounds an octave deeper.

The expression "feet" of tone is derived from this basis.

Any instrument which sounds its tone an octave lower than written in the music, is said to be an instrument of sixteen (16) feet tone.

An instrument which sounds its tones as written, is called an instrument of eight (8) feet tone, whilst an instrument which sounds an octave higher than its tones are written is called an instrument of four (4) feet tone.

The guitar sounds really in the bass clef, but fur convenience sake is noted in the treble clef an octave higher than its tones sound, and hence is an instrument of sixteen (16) feet tone. The violin sounds as written, and is therefore called an instrument of eight feet tone.

The banjo, originally, was an instrument like the guitar, of sixteen feet tone.

### DIVISIONS OF THE SCALE.

If we take a bar of iron and cut it in two, either half will sound an octave above the whole. (it is presupposed that the bar is of even thickness and density throughout.)

I will say, for instance, that the bar sounds the note **C**, in its full length. Now, I have a number of such bars, or rods, all of the same length, thickness and weight, and I wish to construct from them the notes of the diatonic scale in C major. I proceed to cut them up in the following manner:

For C I have the whole bar.

For the next note; D, I cut off one-ninth, leaving eight-ninths.

For E I cut off one-fifth, leaving four-fifths.

For F I cut off one-quarter, leaving three-quarters

For G I cut off one-third, leaving two-thirds.

For A I cut off two-fifths, leaving three-fifths.

For B I cut off seven-fifteenths, leaving eight-fifteenths.

And for the remaining note, C, an octave higher than the first, I cut a bar in half, using either half.

If the bars are, as I have said, perfectly even and equal in thickness throughout, and I have cut them accurately, I have the eight tones, or the seven different sounds, and the octave of the first, quite accurate.

The same will apply to any bar of metal treated in a similar manner, and the same law governs the divisions of musical strings in laying out a fret board for any instrument.

But, as I have said before, *if* a string is " false," which is often the case, the law of divisions is set at defiance.

The higher a note is, the greater the number of vibrations produced.

When vibrations are measured, they are counted at so many vibrations in a second of time. This is done for convenience sake.

A note having twice the number of vibrations produced by another note sounds an octave higher in pitch.

The middle C, years ago, was the note which produced 256 vibrations per second. Now, the middle C, is said to produce about 260 vibrations per second, the standard of pitch having been raised somewhat.

An instrument called a sonometer has been devised for testing and measuring the sounds or tones produced by stretched strings.

It is a very simple affair, consisting of a string stretched over a box, to which weights are attached, with a movable bridge.

The laws governing stretched strings have been ascertained and tested by experimenters in acoustics by means of this sonometer (meaning sound measure).

The rate of vibration of a string is always in *inverse* proportion to its length. That is, as I have stated, a string when vibrated in half its length will sound an octave above the string when vibrated in its whole length; as half the string will produce twice I as many vibrations per second as the whole string. By vibrating a third or a fourth of the string the vibrations become three and four times as fast—*providing the tension is the same.*

Sometimes, when the string is stopped upon a fret, if the string lies any considerable distance from the board, there is a slight change in tension which causes; a somewhat sharp or false note.

A string twice as thick as another will vibrate only half as fast, and consequently sounds an octave lower. This is providing the tension of the two strings is the same. The rate of vibration (so many vibrations per second) is in *inverse* proportion to the strings' thickness. But the strings compared must be of equal density, of course.

Should I replace gut strings upon any instrument, by strings of wire I should use much thinner strings than those of gut; otherwise the change in tension and consequent strain upon the instrument would be enormous.

The rate of a string's vibration is in *inverse* proportion to the square root of the density of the string.

Thus, a gut and a wire string, each the same in length and thickness, and strained to the same tension, will produce entirely different notes. If the wire string is sixteen times as dense as the gut string, the gut string will vibrate four times as fast as the wire string, and the notes produced will sound two octaves above it (four being the square root of sixteen). I have referred to these matters before; you will find them mentioned in my little ten-cent book, "Sketches of Noted Banjo Players," but I cannot allow them to pass here, without making the lecture incomplete.

### FRETS.

It is said that the violin was delayed in its advent for a period of a hundred and fifty years, by frets. The viol, which preceded the violin, was an instrument of *raised frets—on* the same principle in which fretted instruments are made to-day. It was the removal of these frets which led to the developing of the violin and its powers.

188

Owing to this fact some writers on music have thought that the guitar would have done better without the frets also. But I think guitar playing, making chords and barres, on a smooth board, would discourage ninety-nine persons in a hundred from getting further than the first three or four lessons. Playing a guitar without frets is something which is "easier said than done."

I have discussed the subject of fretted banjos at various times in the columns of my *Banjo and Guitar Journal,* and do not wish to go into it at any length here. It has its advantages and it has its disadvantages.

I consider a smooth board by far the most musical, but it requires long and arduous practice to acquire the mastery of.

In short-necked, banjos, such as the *Little Wonder,* and in all "piccolo" banjos, I consider a fretted board preferable; and I might say the same for the *Banjeaurine,* which I manufacture exclusively with the (raised) frets.

It is an important matter for the student to know that if he begins the study and practice of the banjo with a fretted board (when I say "fretted" I mean raised frets, of course), it will be exceedingly difficult for him to acquire a correct intonation afterwards if he should desire to perform upon the smooth unfretted finger-board.

The reason of this is because with frets (raised) the string is pressed to the board between the frets which causes the string to be stopped upon the fret, and hence. an inaccurate and somewhat careless manner of fingering is acquired.

But I fully realize that many pupils would never learn to play upon an unfretted banjo, and I am therefore unwilling to advise all persons to attempt such a task.

Those who intend to practice and play "only a little," would probably do better with frets; but he who intends to devote time to practice and the mastery of the banjo finger-board, should make up his mind to do without such mechanical helps.

### MATHEMATICAL DIVISIONS.

Lord Bacon said: "If a man's wits be wandering, let him study arithmetic." and mathematics, which embraces this study, is probably the only exact science in existence.

Mathematics is inseparable from all other sciences. The physician makes use of it in writing his prescription. The druggist in compounding medicines. The artisan in measuring distances, and the musician in forming his musical bars must measure the notes. Hence, all other sciences are closely allied to and intermingled with this science, and music is in itself an art with a scientific mathematical basis.

### THE CIRCLE AND TRIANGLE

are the emblems of Creation, and the symbols of our mathematical science.

The earth makes its yearly circle around its centre, the sun, and all nature tends to roundness, circles and spiral circles.

Rays of light diverge from the sun and *converge* towards it, the centre, again forming, as it were, the lines of the triangle.

Every musical accord between two notes is defined, and can be expressed *by the arithmetical vibration ratio of two whole numbers.*

By *ratio* is meant the relation which one quantity or magnitude has to another of the same kind.

As has been said, the number of vibrations made by 'a string or other sounding body can be *measured,* and by determining the relation that exists between the *rate of vibration* and the *height of a note,* a mathematical scale for dividing off the frets of an instrument can be made.

It is upon this basis that rules for measuring off guitar and banjo fret-boards have been made.

The rule of consecutive eighteenths is most in use and gives very good results.

The divisions may be made by ordinary arithmetical calculation, always taking care to prove each division by a multiplication before proceeding with the next. A gauge graded to fiftieths and one hundredths of an inch is very useful here, and can be purchased where- ever surveyors' or mathematical instruments are sold.

The divisions may also be made by geometrical progression, but it makes little difference how they are made, so long as they prove correct.

All the various rules laid down for fretting banjos, so far as I have seen, hinge entirely upon the various manners of making the divisions of successive eighteenths, and assume that after you have divided the eighteenths correctly, that you will have an absolutely correct scale of semitones.

But this is a fallacy.

The eighteen is as near as we can get to a number with which to start, but there is nothing to prove that it is absolutely correct.

THIS CHART (from which the accompanying wood cut is a condensed copy) shows a banjo fretting scale divided and set to the triangle.

It will be seen that if we make a correct scale for the longest banjo in use, and it is perfectly adjusted to the triangle, it can be used to fret necks of any desired length.

I first made this chart about seven years ago. I do not claim anything original about it, nor have I ever made any use of it in fretting my banjos.

A is the nutline, and a point of the right angled triangle.

B is the *bridge-line,* and corner of the angle.

C is the remaining point.

The fret divisions must all converge, or run directly to the one point.

By slipping the triangle to the right we can, as has beets said, fret any shorter neck therefrom.

However as there is considerable danger of making mistakes in this way, I advise no one to make use of it.

I give it simply to convey the idea.

Even with a perfectly accurate fret-board a banjo or guitar is often false in many of its notes, simply because strings, which are absolutely true, are scarcely ever to be had.

This is one of the principal objections to raised frets on a long-neck banjo.

A violin virtuoso cuts his string into three pieces, and is generally sure of getting at least one length, which is true; but a banjo artist cannot so cut his strings if he has a banjo of the usual size and proportions.

### THE BANJEAURINE.

This "somewhat different from the ordinary" name is given to this somewhat peculiar-looking instrument. The banjeaurine is a device of my own. It was gotten up as an instrument to be used in connection with the ordinary eleven or twelve-inch banjo; the banjo to play an accompaniment to the melody played upon the banjeaurine.

You will notice that the neck is shorter in length than the diameter of the rim, and that the finger-board of ebony extends over the rim, somewhat similar to that of a guitar or violin. This necessitates the use of a higher bridge than is used on other banjos, and this in itself is a great help to the performer who desires to produce a full, loud tone, and consequently must "pick" the strings vigorously

.

On a low bridge, there being but slight pressure of the strings to resist the upward or side pull by the fingers, the bridge constantly slips Out of place—that is with players of brilliant execution—but with a high bridge, such as can be used upon the banjeaurine, the increased pressure of the strings holds it in position.

Were the instrument intended for "stroke" or thimble playing, the high bridge would not answer so well; but the banjeaurine is not intended or recommended for anything but "guitar style," or picking.

When the instrument was first introduced there was some trouble with the finger-board and neck, and to entirely obviate this I devised the nickel-plated attachment which you see running from the heel of the neck to the end of rim.

This serves as a fastener to the neck, a brace, and also a perfect adjuster of the finger-board.

By turning the screw under the tail-piece nut, the finger-board can be raised or lowered, and to prevent any weakness in the neck a wooden plug is glued into the heel, running directly across the grain and making the neck very strong.

The appearance of the banjeaurine is not calculated to attract a banjo player who has been accustomed to believe that a banjo cannot be good without a neck much longer than the diameter of the rim; but when he has heard it played then he is attracted to it on account of its tone.

It used to be thought that a banjo could not have a full vibration unless the neck was long, and that short neck banjos were not good; but the banjeaurine, although constructed contrary to all previous ideas regarding the instrument, has completely demolished the old theory and, as well, astonished many players of the banjo.

It is much easier to finger than a long neck banjo, because the frets are closer to each other.

It is not so unhandy to transport or carry around

.

It breaks less strings, and is less subject to the annoyances of false strings than a long neck banjo.

It is louder and more brilliant in tone than any other banjo used for "guitar style" of playing, and snakes a beautiful combination with the ordinary banjo, nd is also a splendid solo banjo to play with piano accompaniment.

The banjeaurine is tuned a fourth higher in pitch than an ordinary parlor or Concert banjo, and consequently, when the banjeaurine is played in the key noted as E, the other banjo plays in the key noted as

A. That is the 3d string of the banjeaurine is tuned in unison with the 2d string when stopped at the first fret—or, an octave higher than the bass string open, on the ordinary banjo.

To make it still more simple, I have only to say that when you play in the "open key" on the banjeanrine, the other banjo plays the accompaniment in the "closed key." This explanation is for "ear players."

At the time of introducing the banjeaurine I had not thought of applying for patents in connection with the instrument, but upon being apprised by certain artists who were using the instruments that other makers were preparing to copy the banjeaurine in detail, I then filed    my    application    in    the    patent    office. I suppose it will not be long before I shall hear of other "original Inventors" of my banjeaurine; a thing which has happened in connection with some other devices of my own.

Mr. Huntley, the eminent banjo artist, who has traveled extensively here and in Europe, *and* who has had many years' experience with banjos, assures me that never has he seen, at any time or in any place, an instrument like the banjeaurine, either in appearance or tone.

Mr. Lee, another eminent player and 'writer for the banjo, assures me likewise.

I merely mention these little matters in order to place the origination of the banjeaurine upon record; I don't desire to push the sale of the instrument in place of my legitimate or regular style standard banjos.

# THE CARE OF THE BANJO.

It is necessary to say a few words concerning the proper care of a banjo, as I have found that many players pay but little attention to keeping their instruments in good playing condition.

No machine or instrument ever devised will do good work unless it is kept in proper working condition.

There are some persons who can carry a watch for years and always have it keep good time; others again are never able to rely upon their watches, and often go so far as to expect them to denote the correct time without being wound up.

Briefly, then, I would say that the head of the banjo should always be kept tight, but never held before the fire for the purpose of contracting its fibers. Avoid exposing the instrument to extremes of heat and cold. Avoid keeping the banjo in a damp place; the more even the temperature where the instrument is kept and used, the better its condition.

Always keep an assortment of suitable strings ready for use, and see that your instrument is strung with those of a proper thickness, and properly graded as to size.

The second string should always be a little thicker than the first string; but the fifth, or short string, should be the same thickness as the first.

The bass, or wound string—also called the fourth— should be wound on silk; never upon wire.

The strings should never be slackened after using the instrument; but it is sometimes better to remove or let down the bridge, especially if you are carrying the instrument from place to place.

When the bridge is about to be let down, the first and fifth (or the two outer) strings should be removed from their places in the notches; this will prevent splitting or chipping of the edges of the bridge.

Notches in the bridge should be so cut that the strings wedge in them tight. Then, should the bridge slip out of place when playing, a little powdered rosin may be rubbed upon its feet. The bridge should be regulated in height to each particular banjo; as well as in thickness; and in width to the fingers and tastes of the performer.

The finger-board, strings and neck should be carefully wiped with a silk handkerchief after using the instrument, and a player should never allow an inexperienced person to handle his banjo or to finger the polished surface of the rim and leave finger-marks.

The tail-piece may be fastened with a bolt, with an annealed wire (phosphor bronze wire is the most durable), or with a suitable gut string. It will make no difference in the tone of the instrument how the tail-piece is secured to it, providing it is allowed a certain amount of swing, and does not press upon the head further than at the edge of the rim.

Those who seek to improve the banjo's tone by substituting a gut string for a fastening of annealed wire, are hunting in decidedly the wrong place for the "carrying tone."

The little wedges which secure the neck tightly to the rim in most of the Stewart Banjos should be kept in place properly, and not allowed to become loose or lost out.

I might observe that previous to the use of these: wedges, together 'with the nickel-plated shield or brace, which is screwed to the sound bar in my banjos, that in the majority of banjos the neck was fastened to the rim by screws on each side of the neck, or by a wedge set into the sound-bar.

Since I introduced the shield brace, working in connection with the wedges, some years ago, other manufacturers have taken the idea as a basis for similar devices of their own.

To this I have not the slightest objection; but I have some objection to having my appliances claimed as the inventions of others.

The wedges and shield brace spoken of are not used in the banjeaurine, but only on my Parlor, Concert and Orchestra Banjos. (The Banjo should always be kept in a suitable box or case 'when not in use.)

Another somewhat important thing for a banjo player is to acquire some skill in the handling of the pegs, and in tuning the strings of his instrument; but that properly comes under the head of

# Observations on Banjo **Playing.**

upon 'which subject I shall now endeavor to say a few words. TIME AND SPACE, it is claimed by some writers on metaphysics, exist only in the imagination—within the mind—and yet I feel that I walk in time and live in space.

I wish that time would allow of my going more into the subject of *playing the banjo,* and that space would admit of a more elaborate and detailed lecture upon this branch of my subject.

But I am permitted to give but a brief outline—only a few observations, at present:

Banjo playing is an art—just as much so as violin playing, piano playing, or singing.

The old time "Hop sic doodendo" school of players are passing away. The graceful waltz, polka, schottische, gavotte, concerto and variations on themes, etc., is rapidly superseding the old "Plunk" methods of banjo playing.

A violin in the hands of a scraping and rasping fiddler is not a pleasing instrument to listen to, but sometimes almost infernal. The violin in the hands of the virtuoso is almost supernal. A banjo in the hands of the old time "plunker" is almost as unattractive as the violin in the hands of the rasper and scraper.

And yet the banjo in the hands of a Hall, Huntley, Lee, Powers,

Weston, Henning or Shortis produces music so attractive as to have drawn thousands into its sphere.

There is no telling to what extent perfection in the art of banjo playing may yet be reached.

With suitable books of instruction, and with a proportionate increase in the number of competent teachers, and with suitable banjo literature, banjo playing bids fair to become one of the higher arts.

As time has worked its evolution in the banjo as an instrument, so has it worked its changes in the manner of playing upon it, and in the character of its music.

The old style "stroke," also called "thimble playing," is fast giving way to the guitar style, also called "picking."

The stroke style, the execution of which is done entirely with the forefinger and thumb, was originally the "Old Dan Tucker," "Walk Along, John," plantation negro style of banjo playing; not recognized today by the higher grades of banjo players, but nevertheless useful in creating a little fun and hilarity, and therefore continues to have a place in the repertoire of many players.

But the stroke style has also developed, with practice, by some players, into a very excellent style or method of executing marches or other music of a military type. To play well upon the banjo "with a thimble" (the thimble covers the nail of forefinger and is used to strike the string), and to execute rapid runs and other effects such as "the roll," etc., is no easy object to be attained; and to acquire skill and dexterity in the use of the thimble, a banjoist must practice as diligently as to acquire the same degree of skill in playing guitar style.

Thimble playing is not, as many of you may suppose, merely a rough, unmusical hammering of the strings and head; but maybe developed by practice, into an artistic and pleasing musical performance.

But the number of musical compositions which sound well, or are applicable to this method of performance, are rather small when compared with the compositions and adaptations which are applicable to the guitar style; and the continued practice essential to acquiring a smooth and pleasing execution of the music is often a damper upon the ardor of the aspiring student.

Nevertheless, I have had the pleasure of hearing some excellent music played with the thimble; but on the whole, I prefer the guitar style of playing.

The guitar style of banjo playing, taught in all modern books of instruction, is the style for the parlor as well as for the concert room.

It is equally well adapted to the lady and gentlemen performers.

In executing music, the little finger of the right hand rests upon the head, and the remaining fingers are used to pick the strings.

The further from the bridge the strings are picked, the softer and more lute-like the tone will be.

The ends of the fingers may suffer at first, by continued practice, from the friction of the strings, and become sore and even blister; but in time they become hard and callous, which is essential to a brilliant execution.

Too much practice at the beginning is not recommended, as it is better to practice but a short time at first, and gradually increase, as the muscles of the arm and the ligaments of the fingers become accustomed to and formed to the work.

The pupil should aim to produce a clear tone, distinct, staccato, and, if raised frets are not used, he should endeavor to finger as accurately (with the left hand) as his senses of hearing and feeling will allow.

The sense of sight is also to be used to a certain extent in banjo playing in order to measure distances —to see the finger-board and its                                                                         positions.

The senses of sight and feeling may, by practice, be cultivated and developed, just as the mind or muscular system may be developed.

The sense of hearing, especially the hearing of musical sounds, varies greatly in power and extent in different persons, and may, like other senses, be developed and greatly increased in scope by the right kind of practice.

In practice, when tuning your instrument, I should advise against the strong picking or loud sounding of the strings when they are being brought into tune. Any greater volume of sound than is necessary in order to be distinctly heard, is entirely useless, and often tiresome and offensive to the sensitive ear. The hearing *may* be affected, in some persons, by loud, constant tuning, raising and lowering the pitch of strings, confliction and confusion of sound waves.

The banjo is an instrument that goes out of tune easily; but so is the harp.

Slight changes in temperature effect all the strings, and this fact renders constant tuning necessary. But it may be done in such a quiet way as scarcely to be heard by auditors.

The proper working of the pegs should become part of the early instruction of pupils.

The pegs should be handled gracefully. Do not grasp the banjo neck with the right hand and shove the peg upwards with the left, but take the peg to be tuned, between the thumb and first finger of the left hand, passing the second finger over the top of the peg-head, or scroll; this will allow you to turn the peg with ease, and also afford sufficient pressure to hold it in place.

If pegs are properly tapered and fitted to the holes they are not apt to slip if properly handled.

Machine heads or pegs with cog-wheels, such as are used in most guitars, are about the most provoking and useless article a banjo player could adopt, by reason of being tedious to tune, etc. They are very well for the thick strings of the guitar.

I would also recommend the pupil to sit in as natural a manner as possible while playing. A position which *is* natural to one person may be unnatural to another.

I would also advise pupils and young players to cultivate harmony in and between themselves, and shun the association of those who have no desire to progress, or those who are constantly at *war* with good sense and taste, by bragging about their own wonderful talents and of their powers as banjo players, and how they can "knock out" some one else, or "down" this and "drown out" that.

Such people are as useless to you as they are to the advancement of the art of banjo playing. Their arguments are, in many instances, only to be answered by silent Contempt, and their egotistical self-esteem and assumption of pomp is frequently based upon, or borders upon idiocy.

The law of affinity, or, "like attracts, like," applies to banjo players at well as to others. Where you find one "knocker" you will find more.

I have been accused of speaking harshly about "ear players," by which is meant those who do not read music, but when I have spoken against the practice of playing by ear, it has been more because I considered it a duty than because I would be benefitted in any way.

It was a terrible thing to think about; all these poor heathens, growing up in ignorance of music, and nobody to put them on the right track for fear of offending their royal highnesses.

So instead of spending my spare cash in sending missionaries to Honolulu to teach the poor heathen there how to be good, like us dear Christians in America, I concluded to do what I could to convert the poor heathen in my own country who were growing up in ignorance of the science and art of music.

I may have made some enemies, but I have made many friends among those who have a natural love for the banjo. It is not always possible to convince a man that it is better to study "regular music" than to attempt to learn to play by" ear," or by "simple method," so called. It requires some knowledge of music to be able to appreciate it as a study.

Real music is an intellectual enjoyment, far removed from the rough, uncouth "knocking out" style of barroom banjo players.

It is not always possible to explain to the schoolboy how and why the studies of arithmetic and mathematics will benefit him in after life; he does not "see the use of it." Of course not; nobody can understand or perceive anything that is beyond their mental development. But by progressing with his studies the boy learns how to appreciate and understand. Just so it is with music and banjo players. A study of the scales, with practice, *and* a study of chords, transpositions, etc., develops the mind, and at the same time cultivates the musical ear.

There is no such thing as being really perfect in anything; we are all of us traveling in circles; we see what appears to be the limit of our minds' conception the summit of our ambition—the fullness of our ideal. But as we approach nearer, it seems to recede, and as we appear to get nearer we find other limits far beyond our previous conceptions. Thus it is with the study of any art or science, music and the banjo included. However high you may have progressed in the art of banjo playing, you may yet go higher. The banjo has more in it than has yet been brought out, and it remains for you to further develop it.

Study your instrument well; learn all its points; study music; practice assiduously, and aim for the top. Do not be discouraged if you do not progress as fast as you think you should at first, for at each step of the ladder comes redoubled power to proceed.

If you have a friend who is not so far progressed in music as yourself, it is well for you to show him what you can do and how he may follow; or to aid him in his studies and practice; for in so doing you will also: learn something new for yourself.

Don't think, if you have learned a new piece, that you are the only one who can play it, or that nobody can get it but yourself; for if you so think you will often find yourself mistaken, and perhaps be humiliated. Only small-minded people are bigoted and egotistical; it remains for you to be liberal. If you think you have ideas of your *own,* demonstrate them. If you think you have abilities which no other man who walks the earth possesses, show them up—let us see what you can do. But never brag about what you can do; do it first, then, perhaps, if it amounts to anything, you may have friends who will do all the bragging you need.

If you are so constituted that " taffy" is as necessary to your existence as chicken-feed is to a hen, it maybe better to employ some able person to follow behind and "taffy" you up every now and then.

But if you are told that you are the "best banjo player in the whole world," don't allow that to puff I you up too much, for the same person who tells you that to your face may be so uncharitable as to say, behind your back, that you are the" worst ever

Therefore I advise you to be as even tempered as the musical scale, neither too sharp nor too flat, but of a happy medium.

I have always likened the "ear player" to a mariner who attempts to navigate the deep without rudder or compass. Those who only desire to "play a little," may do as well, perhaps, without notes; but he who desires to progress should learn to, at least, read music.

I fancy that I would rather not listen to a quartette of ear players; if each were to take a different chord at one time it would not be musical.

Those who have studied their chords, scales, etc., *have* some foundation to work upon, even if they do not play everything from the notes.

A few words more and I am finished.

## CONCLUDING REMARKS.
## WARPED RIMS.

No machine has ever been devised to save both time and force; one must be gained at the other's expense. Sometimes a banjo rim will have a tendency to go out of shape, or "warp," and it generally happens in banjos of superior tone.

How often we find men gifted with superior talents In one direction and addicted to some degrading habit in another.

Superior talents are often balanced by some defect, either physical or moral, in the person possessing them.

This is so frequently found to be the case that we might almost call it a law of "second nature."

In some of the very finest old violins it has been found that the backs or tops were often made of patched wood. Doubtless many buyers of cheap violins, to-day, would reject such an instrument, thinking it a "botch."

But the real fact is that the time occupied by those old masters in "patching" that wood would have been sufficient to have allowed them to make at least two or three violins in the ordinary way.

Then why did they so make them?

The reason is said to have been because the wood so used contained peculiar acoustic properties which were seldom to be found, and they used every particle of the wood possible

.

Horace Weston once told me that in his old Clarke's Banjo the rim "warped" to such an extent that he used to be compelled to block the rim when putting a new head on.

And my experience has shown me that when rims are found to go out of shape it is nearly always in banjos possessing a superior tone; but of course there are exceptions to all rules.

In a large instrument of my manufacture, used by Horace Weston, the rim was found to be considerably "Out of round" when brought to me after a year's traveling through the country. I removed the head and after allowing the rim to remain headless over night, found that it had come back to its circle without mechanical aid. So it has been with others.

But some rims will go a little out of shape and stay there, and if the banjo sounds well I recommend their being left just as they are.

In some of the highest-priced guitars the wood is so light and old, and blockings so delicate, that no artist possessing such an instrument would think of allowing it to lie around without a case, or of taking it out of a hot room into the street in the depth of winter. For if it were so used it would speedily crack and become worthless. A banjo player should he as careful of his fine banjo as a guitarist of his guitar, or a violinist of his violin.

Various devices have been formed for the purpose of holding banjo rims round, but it is nearly always the case that form is retained at the expense of tone. For, as I said before, some of the best sounding banjos are those with rims out of shape.

One mechanic will insert a steel (cast) ring inside the rim to hold it round; another a thick band of wood, and another will think that a banjo should have a brass head and steel strings; but, as for myself I prefer the sensitive rim with a good tone; and if I had a rim not wore than a half inch out I should not bother about it; but if the rim was eleven inches one way and thirteen the other, when it should be twelve inches "all ways," I should have it fixed. WARPED NECKS are worse than warped rims; they affect the entire instrument, and if I must have either I prefer the warped rim.

A neck may warp downwards and cause the strings to jar upon the finger-board. It may spring upwards and cause the strings to lie too far away from the board, thus making left-handed fingering very much more difficult.

Necks made with thick finger-boards frequently act in this way, owing to the different shrinkage capacities of the woods used in the neck.

Some makers claim that if the wood is well seasoned the necks will not warp or spring; but this is a fallacy, as some woods, particularly certain grades of walnut, never season so as to be free from warping.

Other makers claim that if the wood is cut so that the grain runs in a certain way that the necks cannot warp; hut this is another fallacy; for the necks so made will warp sideways or twist; just as readily as the same wood would warp in another direction if differently cut.

Only long experience and observation will teach a manufacturer how to avoid these troubles with banjo necks, which, owing to greater length, are more liable to warp than the necks of other instruments.

Again, some players demand necks made so extremely thin that they lack sufficient firmness to stand the strain of the strings, etc.

## HEADS.

When I first went into the business I used to hear considerable about "slunk heads," but I don't hear much about them any more.

Banjo players must be becoming more enlightened, or else a more intelligent class of people is taking hold of the instrument.

Banjo heads are made from the skins of young calves. "Slunk heads" are supposed to be those made from the skins of calves so young as never to have seen the light—that is, still-born calves. Such heads are worthless on a banjo.

Choose a good stiff, partly white head, one of even thickness. When you put it on the rim wet it enough to make it pliable. Let it get well dry before straining.

It does not matter how wet the head is, providing you give it time to dry thoroughly before putting it to a strain; but the wetter the head is made the longer it will require to dry.

Indirect sun-light, in the open air is the shortest and best way to dry a head. The weather, of course, must be clear when exposed.

Some amateurs have a predilection for heads that are all transparent (such skins used to be used in place of glass, for windows, in olden times), and others think only such as are "all white" can be good; but the knowing ones, i. e., experienced players, select their heads with regard to other properties than color, knowing that artificially prepared heads are often weak in strength as well as in sonorousness. The head is the most sensitive part of the instrument, and the more uniform in density the air, and the less variable the climate, the better.

And now for the lack of those important factors, time and space. I must close, hoping to go deeper into the subject at some future time, however remote.

NOTE.—The foregoing lecture is given just as originally written; with perhaps many imperfections, errors and omissions. It is scarcely possible to cover the ground of such a subject in a few words and at the same time be clear and comprehensive; and at present I have not the time to devote to a more elaborate and detailed analysis of the various points introduced; neither have I the desire to employ any one to "write up" my lectures or other articles, from memoranda supplied by myself, as is done by many.

Therefore, the lecture, such as it is, is given to the public just as it proceeds from my pen—without elaboration—without any pretention to rhetorical style, and I hope without perplexing mystifications.

In short, what I have said, is intended for the rising school of banjo players—*banjoists,* notwithstanding the omission of the word from Webster's dictionary —not for the critics.

## THE BRIDGE.

The following cuts, or diagrams, give in outline the size of bridges generally used on the banjeaurine and banjo.

Diagram A, represents the banjeaurine bridge; Diagram B, the banjo bridge.

Taking the centre of the bridge as the place to notch for the third string, we make a circle from this centre for the positions of the two outer strings, and then setting the dividers one-half shorter, we form another circle from same centre for the two remaining notches.

Made in the USA
Middletown, DE
30 September 2023

39526317R00119